TORAH OF THE STREET, TORAH OF THE HEART
Copyright © 2016 by Rabbi Dr. Shmuly Yanklowitz. No part of this book may be used or reproduced in any manner whatsoever without permission, unless in the cases of brief quotation, excerpting, critical review, and articles. All rights reserved.

FIRST EDITION
Summer 2016

Designed by Abraham J. Frost

Typeset in Baskerville & Strong Glasgow

FRONT COVER AND BACK COVER DETAIL ILLUSTRATION: *March on Washington for Jobs and Freedom, August 28, 1963.* THIS WORK WAS OBTAINED FROM THE NOW DEFUNCT UNITED STATES INFORMATION AGENCY. IN 1999 THE AGENCY WAS MERGED INTO THE BUREAU OF PUBLIC AFFAIRS WHICH IS PART OF THE UNITED STATES DEPARTMENT OF STATE. THIS WORK IS IN THE PUBLIC DOMAIN IN THE UNITED STATES BECAUSE IT IS A WORK OF THE UNITED STATES FEDERAL GOVERNMENT UNDER THE TERMS OF 17 U.S.C. § 105.

ISBN-13: 978-1535584548
ISBN-10: 1535584548

OTHER WORKS BY RABBI DR. SHMULY YANKLOWITZ

Existing Eternally, Existing Tomorrow

The Jewish Vegan (Ed.)

SPARKS! Bringing Light Back Into The World

*Soul Searching:
A Jewish Workbook For Spiritual Exploration And Growth*

*Bringing Heaven Down To Earth:
Jewish Ethics For A Complex And Evolving World*

*Spiritual Courage:
Vignettes On Jewish Leadership For The
Twenty-First Century*

The Soul Of Jewish Social Justice

Epistemic Development In Talmud Study

*Jewish Ethics & Social Justice:
A Guide For The 21st Century*

Torah of the Street
Torah of the Heart

Torah of the Street
Torah of the Heart

Essays on Jewish Activism, Spirituality, Social Justice, and Ethics

Rabbi Dr. Shmuly Yanklowitz

© 2016

THIS BOOK IS DEDICATED TO SHOSHANA, AMIELLA, AND LEV
YOU FILL MY HEART WITH JOY, BLESSINGS, AND LOVE.

Contents

Introduction

I. Ritual & Spirituality

1. Ritual's Power to Transform — 7
2. The Mandate to be Spiritually Destructive?
   Rav Kook's "Holiness that Destroys" — 9
3. Were Adam and Eve Black Transgender Refugees? — 11
4. Having a Wills Party?
   Preparing for the Future — 14
5. A Case for *Yom Tov Sheni* — 17
6. Young People Chasing Atheism?
   The Breakdown of Modern Religion — 19
7. The Secret To Jewish Survival — 22

II. Theology

1. Help! I Am Becoming a Panentheist:
   An Open Letter to Rav Kook — 29
2. Why Was the Torah Revealed Outside of Israel? — 32

3 Was Revelation a Divine Compromise?	35
4 An Open Letter to Baruch Spinoza	38
5 Developing a Second *Halakhah*	40
6 The Rebbe of Gur & the Power of Now	43

III. Leadership

1 Rabbi Yitz Greenberg's *Sage Advice*	49
2 Learning Leadership From the Bible, Harvard and a Chief Rabbi	51
3 Standing Together In the Era of National Division: Review of *United* by Senator Cory Booker	54
4 A Review of Zakheim's *Nehemiah: Statesman and Sage*	58
5 Bold Protest or Blind Faith?	61

IV. Social Justice

1 See the Invisible People: The Hidden Cry of Our Generation	67
2 The Urgent Need for a Living Wage	70
3 Jewish Leaders Take A Stand Against The Death Penalty	73

4	ZUCKERBERG & CLINTON: A Jewish Perspective of Altruism	77
5	When Activists Hijack Campaigns, Vital Causes Suffer	80
6	The Most Powerful and The Most Vulnerable	83
7	Student Debt Crisis: Make College Free	85
8	Angels, Men and Government: Bringing Civility Back to the Political Discourse	89
9	Can Religious Institutions Become Sweeping Forces for Social Progress?	92
10	The World is Still Flooding	95
11	A Plea for the Citizens of Syria	97
12	*Parshat Shoftim*: Just Courts or More Than Just Courts?	99
13	The Religious Imperative to Oppose Solitary Confinement	101
14	How To Combat Hate In Society	104

V. Kidney Donation

1	Give a Kidney, Get a Check	109

2 WE BADLY NEED MORE   112
   DONATED KIDNEYS.
   LET'S START PAYING FOR THEM

VI. Animal Welfare

1 AN INTERFAITH COMPASSION   117
   MOVEMENT CAN CHANGE THE
   WORLD

2 DO ANIMALS HAVE LEGAL RIGHTS?   120

3 ON THE EXTINCTION OF ANIMALS,   124
   CLIMATE CHANGE, &
   SHILUACH HA'KAN

4 DO YOU BLUSH?   126
   OUR INNER LIGHT AS SPIRITUAL ANIMALS

5 A SPIRITUAL PERSPECTIVE   128
   ON A PLANT-BASED DIET

VII. Interfaith Partnerships

1 A GATHERING OF GLOBAL FAITH   135
   LEADERS:
   MY EXPERIENCE AT THE PARLIAMENT OF
   WORLD RELIGIONS

2 TOWARDS JEWISH-CHRISTIAN   137
   RECONCILIATION & PARTNERSHIP

VIII. Within the Orthodox Community

1. Why We Should Stop Bashing the Ultra-Orthodox Community — 143
2. Can Orthodoxy Get Back On Track? — 146
3. The Chief Rabbinate: *Tzimtzum* and *Hitpashtut* — 149
4. Orthodoxy Should Embrace Interfaith Families — 152
5. Religious Pedagogues Should Embrace Liberal Education — 157

IX. Personal Growth & Relationships

1. Spiritual Awakenings: Learning to Trust Ourselves — 165
2. Are You Prepared to Reject Seduction? Strengthening our Families — 167
3. Can We Resurrect the Virtue of Friendship in Our Time? — 169
4. Enough With the Million Dollar Birthday Parties — 172
5. Bringing Kindness Into the Workplace — 176

6	ARE WE RESPONSIBLE FOR ONE ANOTHER?	179
7	WELCOMING YOUNG LEADERS TO BOARDS	181
8	THE EMOTIONAL ROLLER COASTER OF FOSTERING A CHILD	183

CONCLUSION

ACKNOWLEDGMENTS

This book consists of essays originally published in: *Jewish News of Greater Phoenix*, *Forks Over Knives*, *Huffington Post*, *Times of Israel*, *Jewish Journal* (Los Angeles), the *Jerusalem Post*, *Newsweek*, *The Atlantic*, *The Guardian*, *Phoenix New Times*, and *Modern Loss*, among other publications. It is my hope that the ideas contained in this book will help inspire readers to continue to do the hard work of taking spiritual activism and translating it into meaningful action.

I'm so thankful for the diligent editing work of Abraham J. Frost and Dr. Peter Geidel.

I'm ever grateful to my supportive and loving wife Shoshana, and our children, Amiella and Lev. Thank you for all the love and inspiration you share with me every day.

I thank the Creator for giving me strength, wisdom, and infusing my life with holy purpose.

INTRODUCTION

I believe in Torah. I believe in its truths, its depths, and its ability to alter the fabric of society. To say that *Torah*, as an all-encompassing universe for Judaism's epistemological enterprise, is the most central piece of religious pedagogy ever written is an understatement. No other document in human history has had such an effect on the destinies of nations, on the aspirations of the weak and powerful alike. Morals and ethical movements find their home in Torah. Societies have been built on the foundations of Torah; mendicants and kings alike find succor in the stories of Abraham, Moses, David, Solomon, Ruth, and Esther.

The notion that religion has a place in the modern society is declining rapidly; this is a widespread, immediate, and real impression felt by many across the globe. For too long, religion has become an institution of suspicion rather than inspiration. Due to the infuriating influx of rigid fundamentalism, coercive communities, and violence perpetrated in the name of theology, we have good reason to be skeptical of scriptures and clerical demagogues. Yet, even as there seems to be an irrevocable slide towards absolutism, we are also witnessing a great reformation where faith traditions are looking inward, engaging in the great re-interpretation of their core being, and ensuring that the ethical needs of the soul take primacy. And yet, if all this is true, why does it seem that the modern world is falling behind in its ethical pursuits?

It is in this woeful leadership vacuum caused by societal lethargy where our vision emerges. It is in this gap where we can undertake any challenge that comes our way. Our tasks—so immediate and vital—are to *expand* our own consciousness to hear more vulnerable voices, to deepen our sensitivities, and reinvigorate our sense of living in a united community built upon respect for diversity. The ancient wisdom of how to achieve this ideal is hanging before our eyes, but it must be grappled with and adapted to remain relevant. To engender transformation in the world, the hallowed traditions we share should not remain stagnant nor evolve too quickly. They need to be challenged, they need to be ruminated upon seriously; we should avoid being too radical or too reactionary in our leadership.

This lack of action applies—sadly—to contemporary Judaism. In the Jewish community today, we see more and more Jews turning off the complexity of their tradition. Many have watered it down, thrown out meaningful observance, and have disregarded particularism and a rigorous spiritual path; they have merely embraced a simple universalistic version of their birthright. On the other side of the spectrum, many have turned off the intricacy and multiplicity of viewpoints found throughout the thousands of years of our history for the supposed simplicity of perceived "righteous" observance.

Yet when it comes to pressing matters of ethics and social justice in our time, urgency is the name of the game. The Torah must not hold us back but propel us forward to lead on these crucial matters. We must be reflective and intentional but also move with zeal and fervency. It must learn the Torah of the heart and the Torah of the streets. For the Divine word to be alive it must be pervasive and ubiquitous. We must speak to our personal lives and our public lives, transforming ourselves and all involved for the better.

Can Judaism rise above the myopia of modern societal decadence? Can the Jewish people lead and foster a sustained, compassionate world? Can we hold onto our deep particularistic tradition with great rigor while remaining deeply committed to the humble pluralism that embraces the truth wherever it can be found?

Confronting the enormous issues in our time requires that they are to be debated honestly and openly by everyone. In *Torah of the Street, Torah of the Heart,* I approach these deep questions with an eye toward their difficult, open-ended nature to the best of my ability. My intention with this book is to start a conversation. My hope is that you'll feel challenged and you'll be enlightened, you may get upset and you may walk away hopeful by the following pages. Whatever the case, it is my hope that you come away with the inspiration to go out into the world and make it a better place. However you choose to do this, let us do it with all of our souls.

And let us do it together.

Ritual & Spirituality

1.
Ritual's Power to Transform

Every morning, I wake up to an inbox full of dozens of emails, global news demanding reaction, and a daily agenda triple the size of what will prove achievable. How am I to pause and turn inward? When I put on my *tefillin* each morning, I fully consider what I need to become liberated from in order to return to my highest callings; the straps bind me to my sacred mission.

Rituals are non-utilitarian: symbolic acts that involve and promote the cultivation of mindfulness. The transformative power of ritual is achieved when we take the opportunity to explore ourselves, our hearts and our ideals. We step out of this world to cultivate a meaningful experience and then to return to life changed. This is why we seek to perform ritual on our own and not by proxy. There are multiple explanations for—and values to—the performance of ritual. *Ritual*, in its essence and spelling, is the root of *spiritual* because we can only really access the depths of our minds, hearts, and souls when we consistently perform certain physical acts with our bodies. Rambam explained that the deepest human learning comes from habituation.

Returning to ritual each day of our lives helps condition us to live by these ideals. Some explain that the great power of ritual is social since the performance of rituals indicates commitment to a group and to an identity. Ritual adds stability to a community and tightens social bonds through the sharing of meaningful practices. Others suggest that ritual allows for catharsis—emotional purging—since in ritual one can emotionally distance oneself from certain life events and experience feelings with some separation.

The danger in ritual is that one can use the power of the structure to avoid internalization. One can sit *shiva* as their act of mourning, yet never truly embrace the grief and loss. One could embrace *kashrut* (kosher consumption), yet never seek the deeper spiritual and ethical components to the ritual. One could pray from a *siddur* every day, yet never really concentrate on the deeper meaning of the words re-cited. Ritual, at its worst, distracts us from real life. But, at its best, ritual can enhance the mindfulness with which we live.

The laws of *kashrut* are perhaps the most ritually dynamic since we encounter food consumption more than any other ritual act each day. Yet, they are the most neglected. How often do we allow our food consumption to go beyond checking the box that to make sure that the contents are kosher? How often to we allow these laws to really stir something in our hearts and conscience and think about how food consumption and *kashrut* is changes us? We merely aren't to satisfy hunger, but to perform the righteous ritual of *kashrut* dozens of times a day.

Not too long ago, I heard Jonathan Safran Foer speak about the "room-servicing of life," how the tendency today is to prefer that others do things for us rather than doing them for ourselves. Ritual is the radical reminder that we live our own lives. The greatest power of religious ritual, in my view, is the opportunity to deepen one's self-awareness about one's own moral and spiritual values. Too rarely do we pause to give birth to the dreams and the visions that make our lives unique. As Erich Fromm wrote: "Man always dies before he is fully born." Ritual gives us the chance to pause, to assess how we are living and to give birth to our spiritual potential. It is to be done with urgency since we never know when our time on this earth will run out, and we will have passed away before we've given birth to our great contributions in this world.

Even further, it reminds us of our ability to slow down. A study in the *Academy of Management Journal* stated that when confronted with clear choices of right and wrong, and when given to think about the issue, rather than make a quick decision, people are five times more likely to do the right thing. Pausing to reflect provides moral clarity.

Daily ritual is an opportunity to pause, reflect and step out of our routine to hear the voice of our inner conscience. Viktor Frankl explained that moral life exists in the moment between stimulus and response. Ritual reconditions us to make more of those crucial moments in our life that elevate us from base to noble and can be used to enhance our psychological processes and internal incentives.

Every year, we return to the Haggadah and the *shofar*. Every week, we return to candle-lighting and Shabbat song. Every day, we return to text study and prayer. These rituals are about religious worship, intellectual development, community-building, and emotional stability. But they are also important for the creation of the just society, ensuring that we all take moments to return to non-utilitarian acts that do not advance our self-interest, but challenge us to stop and listen. In an age of honking, buzzing and texting, this may be one of our greatest moral salvations.

The performance of ritual is the timeless channel back to purpose.

2.
THE MANDATE TO BE SPIRITUALLY DESTRUCTIVE? RAV KOOK'S HOLINESS THAT DESTROYS

The process of growing in a spiritual sense is multifaceted and intricate. Humans are delicate beings and as more aspects of our lives change, the more we may try to impede that change.

It is inevitable. It is human nature.

For most our lives, we become accustomed to a routine—a repetitive narrative—and a familiar self-perception. When the routine is disrupted, it signals a consequential shift in how we cope with foreign experiences. It begins at birth: what rightful person would ever want to leave the warmth and support of the womb? It is this first action of personhood that is the framework for living a life where one can overcome arduous obstacles and take control of their destiny.

All throughout our development, we are given manifold opportunities to expand our horizons, to go out into to the world and devour the competing philosophies that explain the human condition. In these bursts, our knowledge grows, as does the appreciation for the infinite cosmologies that occupy the ether of human potential. But to truly build up our continuing mastery of spiritual development, we have to break the incorrect foundations within us that continually hold us back. In our intellectual pursuits, we must challenge established truths to reach higher truths, provoke our own inner paradigms and mental models, and reach new heights with a perspicacity for knowledge that should never be satiated.

Being spiritually creative is a pretty easy sell. But more imperative to the soul is the mandate to be spiritually destructive. A significant contradiction, no?

No!

Breaking down old norms and revitalizing intellectual pursuits keeps us grounded, dilating our minds for novel ideas and new experiences. Rav Kook explained this value:

"There is a holiness that builds and a holiness that destroys. The benefits of the holiness that builds are visible, while the benefits of the holiness that destroy are hidden, because it destroys in order to build what is nobler than what has been built already. One who understands the secret of the holiness that destroys can mend many souls, and one's capacity for mending is in accordance with one's understanding. From the holiness that destroys there emerge great warriors who bring blessing to the world… One whose spirit cannot reach out to the wide horizons, one who does not search for the truth with their whole heart, cannot tolerate spiritual destruction but neither to do they have any edifices they have built themselves (*Orot HaKodesh* 2:314).

The pursuit of holiness is tantamount to a life well-lived. This is not only true for our inner world but also for all revolutions. A previous societal model has to be destroyed in order for a new and more advanced model to emerge. Pain and loss is involved in drastic change whether it occurs slowly or rapidly. But we feel this in miniature throughout our lives: the interests of a nine-year old can't be the same interests as a thirty year old. In that gap of time, a new person emerges, invigorated from past experiences but ready to face new ones, hopefully with deftness and cunning.

Looking more broadly into Jewish tradition, it is for this reason that the Israelites needed forty years wandering in the desert to transition from being slaves to being a free people. To destroy the old slave mentality requires a fetter being broken; no small matter. And this is what God asks of us each day. Each of us must retreat to the desert to reflect and transition, only to emerge in to our own promised land to live with our new truths.

In my own life, I strive to embrace significant stages in my spiritual development. Over the last few decades I have tried to cultivate each paradigm shift, recognizing that each came with sadness accompanying the joy; not always pleasant but necessary. When we reach a new understanding of Divinity, human interconnectivity, and the dynamism of spiritual maturation, then and only then, can we celebrate our elevated consciousness. We may mourn that the previous relationship with God and the cosmos is now dead, never to be recovered. But we must also rejoice!

The world is filled with a new light and there is no choice but to carry on. We must destroy inner worlds in order to build new ones.

3.
WERE ADAM AND EVE BLACK TRANSGENDER REFUGEES?

When the world was created, darkness and light were incomprehensible concepts. The separation between elements — sky and water, soul and sinew — were not yet formed from the void.

When God finally crafted the Human on the sixth day, the assumption for most students of the Bible is that Man was created first, and from him, Woman was created. This reading is widely accepted and has been taught for centuries, ignoring the other biblical version that they were created simultaneously and interconnected. While it is certainly true that a plain reading of these early biblical passages suggests that the dyad of man and woman was one of the most pertinent intentions of Creation, a closer textual analysis presents another more radical view: the view that identities of gender, sex, race, and ethnicity are not determined by nature but are largely developed as social constructs to make sense of the world. It would be blasphemous for one to apply one's chosen construction of what is "normal" or "natural" to marginalize another. Doing so would be nothing short of challenging the full Divine potential of the first human who subsequently encapsulates all future human natures. Denying that any unique permutation was fully created in the image of God is akin to denying God.

The Hebrew term *Adam* is usually meant to express the idea of male, or male identity. But in the early passages of Genesis, the term is made more contextually ambiguous. To wit, Adam can be discerned as embodying a singular personal concept, or a universal one. Though this would seem contradictory *prima facie*, there is a relevant (though hidden) teaching embedded in the passage, namely that the harmonization of the seemingly contradictory creation of humanity is a sign of a Divine work in which all people are of equal status. Adam comes from *adamah* which simply means earth; all humans emerged from the universal substance of nature.

Thus, Adam and Eve were not only the first human beings, but also the archetypal configurations for ALL of humanity; the social consciousness lessons that emerge from the brief time we come to know these two figures in the Bible is staggering. Indeed, as it can be seen from our contemporary perspective, all descendants came from Adam and Eve, thus also all descendants were contained within them. The diversity of humanity teaches us how complexly rounded Adam and Eve were when they were united as one being. The first human being was black and white, gay and straight, male and female, a citizen of the Garden of Eden and a stateless refugee from the garden, made from heaven and from earth. Each of us, in our own uniqueness, can find ourselves within the first person and thus within the Divine purpose of the creation of humanity.

The rabbis taught that God had a miraculous capacity for creating all humans as descendants from one and yet, concurrently, providing a holy uniqueness within each:

When a human being strikes many coins from one mold, they all resemble one another, but the supreme Sovereign of sovereigns, the Holy One, blessed be God, fashioned every person in the stamp of the first human, and yet not one of them resembles another. For this reason, every human being is obligated to say, "For my sake, the world was created" (Jerusalem Talmud, *Sanhedrin* 4:22).

This is not a trivial point. Shimon Ben Azzai, a second century Jewish explicator, taught that "'This is the genealogy of Adam' is the great principle of the Torah" (Jerusalem Talmud, *Nedarim* 9:41). Understanding that a singular set of beings contained within them all the genetic complexity and spiritual DNA that would later emerge in various manifestations of humanity displays to us that the human dignity found within the first people is innate and infinite in every subsequent person, regardless of their composition or persuasion.

How all this biblical material relates to contemporary events is of the utmost importance. I fear that today, with the lingering effects of racism, xenophobia, and the stigmatization of gay and trans people, humanity is still needlessly looking for reasons to divide itself. While I may not understand or approve the underlying reasons why each person chooses their particular lifestyle, as a Modern Orthodox pluralistic rabbi guided by the Torah, I feel it is my obligation to seek out those who are most vulnerable and advocate on their behalf. It is not enough to tolerate differences, but to cherish and nurture individuals so that they have the fortitude to go out into the world to live an actualized life. The *raison d'être* of the Torah is to enhance human dignity and freedom and never—God forbid—to diminish it.

Diversity is not something to push back against in the name of human uniformity. Rather, one of the vital acts we can do is reach out to someone struggling with their identity and give them the space to flourish. Too often, societies have pushed away those who grapple with their inner selves, even cutting them off from the broader world. Our post-modern globalized systems of interaction necessitate that the connection between humans is now weaker than ever.

We can bring much kindness and justice back into the world, if we embrace the opportunity, indeed imperative, to support those who are suffering from marginalization and shaming. Indeed, it stems from our ancient mandate of giving aid to the stranger, giving succor to the weak, and being kind to all. And in doing so, we embrace the notion that all of us were contained in God's first human creation. This makes each of us all equal yet—paradoxically—completely unique.

4.
HAVING A WILLS PARTY?
PREPARING FOR THE FUTURE

"A man cannot say to the Angel of Death, 'Wait till I make up my accounts'"
- *Ecclesiastes Rabbah* 8:11

Not too long ago, after months of conversations and moral deliberations, my wife and I finalized our wills. To mark the occasion, we threw a "wills party," wherein we signed our wills in front of our witnesses and a notary. Afterward, my wife and I reflected on the importance of what we had just done: We came away with the feeling that, while we certainly strive to live responsibly, it would also be severely thoughtless of us to die irresponsibly.

When my wife and I threw our wills party, we were cognizant of the serious project we had completed. It was an imperative, but a practical one for the benefit of our family. Going through the process of creating a will was both melancholic, but also a little joyful: Here you are with your family and friends celebrating a life you hope will be long and fruitful.

It's also a contemplative experience.

Consider these questions: How much of any remaining assets will go to which family members? How much to charity? How much life insurance (if any) should be bought? What medical instructions should be given for any precarious end-of-life situations? And at what point should organs be donated? Who should raise the children if both parents die before children are grown up? These questions are difficult and painful to consider, especially for those of us with young children. We dare not run away from them.

And yet, too many Americans do (and not only young families). A recent legal service survey showed that more than half of Americans age 55-64, and more than 60 percent of people in the United States between the ages 45-54, have no will. More than half of survey participants admitted to procrastination; meanwhile 40 percent thought that either a will wasn't important or that they didn't need one. About 1 in 7 had avoided making a will because they did not want to contemplate their own mortality. In a notable case, the rock musician Prince passed suddenly without drafting a will, thereby causing the affairs of his estate in contention with many claimants for his vast fortune.

People who die without a will—intestate—will have their estate distribution determined (often by the local surrogate court) in formulas worked out by each state.

One myth that must be dispelled is that the federal government will take much of one's estate after death. The federal estate tax—a.k.a. the "death tax"—affects only a single person whose estate is worth $5.45 million (or a couple with more than $10.9 million), which accounts for about 1 in 500 Americans. As for small businesses and farms, only about 20 percent pay any federal estate tax annually. On the state level, about sixteen states charge estate taxes, and all but New Jersey have exemptions of at least $1 million. In addition, about a half dozen states collect inheritance taxes. Spouses are exempt from taxation, and descendants are in most cases also exempt, but others are almost always not exempt, and the rates can vary from 1 percent to 20 percent; Maryland and New Jersey are the only two states to collect an inheritance tax and an estate tax.

Of course, one could include a charity as a beneficiary, which is tax deductible and can continue to do good after one's death. One study, using self-reported data from the Health and Retirement Study, indicated that only about 10 percent of Americans with a will or trust included a charity as a beneficiary in 2010.

Creating a will—planning for the end of your life—is in and of itself, an unremarkable venture. It is only but another legal document, another meeting with an attorney, another visit with our own mortality that we bind ourselves with. But it doesn't have to be relegated to the back of our minds.

For my wife and me, setting the terms of our will was an exercise in thinking about our life together, all the pitfalls and peaks of parenthood, all the memories that have yet to be created. The minute we set about having a party after signing a will, it was a moment where we seriously celebrated the love we share for each other, our children, and, paradoxically, life itself. We knew our decisions were not final (as one can add codicils with updates and changes); nonetheless, we took serious steps forward together.

Death is such a multifaceted endeavor. Meditating on our ultimate fate is undeniably difficult. For us to comprehend how we are capable of facing it takes a type of courage that is hard to muster. What is certain, however, is that we need to be prepared emotionally, financially, medically, relationally, and spiritually: We need to consider how we will die (emotionally), how we will leave our estates (financially), how we will leave our bodies (medically), how we will leave our families (relationally), and how we will prepare for post-life (spiritually).

This process may not be pleasant, but it is essential. But it is not the end of the discussion. Rather, it's another beginning. And who doesn't love an excuse to throw a party, especially one where we celebrate the good things we have in life?

5.
A Case for Yom Tov Sheni

There seems to be some talk in the Modern Orthodox community today about dropping the second day of *yom tov* (holiday). While I personally enjoy having more days to celebrate these meaningful holidays with my family in spiritual celebration, I can understand these tensions in parts of the community: observance can be challenging for work schedules and other important components of daily living. And for many, the observance of the extra days doesn't make much rational sense anymore. But I feel that these holidays are vital. I want to make a modest case as for why Jews should stay strong in our commitment to keeping two days of *yom tov*.

Yom Tov Sheni has historical origins in a significant problem: there was a lack of certainty as to when *yom tov* would begin (*sfeika d'yoma*). Due to this doubt, the rabbis added a second day (*yom tov sheni shel galuyot*) to be sure we got the day right (*Rosh Hashanah* 22b; *Beitzah* 4a-6a; *Hagigah* 8a-b). In our modern time, we know the correct date, but we as traditional Jews observe two days since it was decreed by the rabbis nonetheless.

My thought experiment: How could this become a holiday with the theme of doubt-celebration? Today, there is such a zealousness for certainty that we blind ourselves to the beauty of what tradition can offer us. Religion's purpose is to inspire awe, to give a sense wonder, and to foster holy doubt; certainty should not be a goal of religion. Inspired by an idea shared by Reb Zalman who says he learned it from Rabbi Meyer Fund, I want to suggest that we can re-embrace *yom tov sheni* based upon the value of doubt/*suffaik* (*Integral Halakhah*, 81).

Rav Kook taught that doubt was built into the universe and that it's crucial for a serious religious life:

When one level seeks to glorify itself in a certainty that oversteps the limits of its own certainty, or desires to draw a certainty fuller and broader than its own writ, than that to which it is internally connected and which it can absorb in itself, then it loses its balance, stumbles and falls, dives into darkness, weaves and strays like a drunk, breaks and explodes. Until from within the darkness light will emerge, and be renewed in a new formation, and its measure of doubt will rise to the fount of certainty, and those who dwell in dust will awake and sing, for your dew is the dew of lights (*Shemoneh Kevatzim* 5:117).

For another view, consider Yehuda Amichai's poem "The Place Where We are Right":

From the place where we are right
flowers will never grow
in the spring.
The place where we are right
is hard and trampled
like a yard.
But doubts and loves
dig up the world
like a mole, a plow.
And a whisper will be heard in the place
where the ruined
house once stood.

Yom Tov Sheni can be the institution that reminds us of our lack of certainty. It startles us from our position of intellectual and spiritual hubris. Because the day was built upon doubt, it can be maintained through doubt. "What am I still doing in *shul* and at the *yom tov* table?" Perhaps, through this observance, we can return religion to its rightful grandeur as a bastion for humility, intellectual curiosity, and spiritual wonder.

6.
Young People Chasing Atheism? The Breakdown of Modern Religion

While I strongly disagree, I have a respect for rational atheism, because there is a cogent argument that can be made for evolution, humans existing alone, no afterlife, and an enlightened secular lifestyle. Sadly, atheists, like Jews, have long suffered for their inherent beliefs. Even today, according to a report by the International Humanist and Ethical Union, fifty-five nations outlaw "blasphemy." Ironically, Russia, which in the Soviet period was the world's most overt atheist state, now supports its Orthodox Christian church by criminalizing blasphemy. In the Islamic world, "apostasy" is outlawed in nineteen countries, and thirteen Islamic states have made blasphemy or apostasy a capital offense. About a dozen countries also have laws that can take away the citizenship of atheists and deny them the right to marry. Even in the United States, supposedly a nation where religious beliefs (or lack thereof) are themselves sacred, Arkansas, Maryland, Mississippi, North Carolina, South Carolina, Tennessee, and Texas still retain (unenforceable) laws on the books barring atheists from holding public office. In the twenty-first century, religious leaders around the world continue to fear and persecute atheists rather than respectfully engage them. Why is there so much fear and anger toward those who arrive at different intellectual and spiritual conclusions?

The notion that holding atheistic beliefs is antithetical to the American ideal is long-held. Thomas Paine, whose eighteenth-century pamphlets *Common Sense* and *The American Crisis* helped create and sustain the American Revolution, was committed to secularism. Whether out of conviction or because he felt he had to say it, Paine wrote that he was a monotheist. Nevertheless, he (and many others of the Founding generation) rejected emphatically all organized religion. Still, his moral convictions reflected a common bond with many devout religious reformers: "I believe that religious duties," he wrote in *Age of Reason*, "consist in doing justice, loving mercy, and endeavoring to make our fellow-creatures happy… My own mind is my own church." Yet, in spite of Paine's efforts to raise moral awareness during the American and French revolutions (unlike some of the other Founding Fathers, his strong opposition to slavery went back as early as 1775), he would later purportedly be dismissed as that "filthy little atheist" by none other than President Theodore Roosevelt.

Despite having an understanding of atheism and secularism from a rationalist's perspective, I don't, however, have a respect for lazy atheism nor, for that matter, lazy religion. Today, many people without a well-defined philosophy of atheism turn towards that direction nonetheless. As a fervent "believer," I feel that a relationship with the Divine has an enormous amount to offer and that we are failing many who seek that relationship. Today, only about 1.5 to 4 percent of Americans admit to being "hard atheists." A much larger number (around 20 percent), have embraced *skepticism* and have completely moved away from organized religion. These so-called "Nones"—aka those committed to no faith—are the fastest-growing "religious" group in America in comparison to the growth of any other faith. They seem to be fleeing religious communities more than they are running toward other forms of enlightenment. Could the religious institutions themselves be at fault for this phenomenon?

Part of the mistake may indeed be religious institutions, especially ones that sociologist David Kinnaman (a devoted Christian) writes are "[N]ot safe and hospitable places to express doubts" (*You Lost Me*, 11). He argues that young Americans today value skepticism, choice, and personal expression and want to steer clear of hierarchy, certainty, and identity barriers that may lead to intolerance. Can twenty-first century religious communities embrace these needs while maintaining their norms and cherished values?

Alternatively, this phenomenon could be attributed to the fact that religious leaders have too drastically moved towards the political extreme, expecting to win cause for their moral pursuits. In doing so, those members many who may be centrists or more liberal are left to feel alienated by religious leadership often advocating more conservative agendas. Robert Putnam and David Campbell argued, in their book *American Grace*, that this religious alienation of the left began in the '90s.

I would suggest though that the main reason atheism, agnosticism, and the move away from organized religion is spreading is due to a perceived lack of immediate relevance of God in our lives. If religious people are not demonstrating that they are more giving, kind, compassionate, and spiritually attuned then they are telling younger generations that belief in God is irrelevant to living a good, meaningful, and successful life. Furthermore, we have long been left without the tools to process the Divine's role in how to lead our lives. We need *big* questions from religion, not simple answers. How does our relationship with God give us more perseverance and hope? How does religion deepen the sanctity of our human relationships? How does faith empower us rather than make us more passive waiting for a miracle? How might our moral imagination and consciousness grow rather than shrink when in a religious community? How do we collectively navigate our conjunctive emotions—those of joy, humility, and compassion—along with our disjunctive emotions like sadness, fear, and loss? These are important, oft-forgotten questions that are vital to our spiritual well-being.

Perhaps—a bit radically—I believe that religious communities and secular humanists are not too far apart in their commitment to making the world a more just place. By cooperating to stimulate people to make spiritual commitments that alleviate enormous problems people face in the world, whether it's income disparity, environmental issues, the un-precedented number of refugees in the Middle East and Africa, or whatever issue seems pressing to the individual, there is much common ground. A religious commitment can give people the spiritual stamina to transcend the apathy and disillusion that is so pervasive in our world.

We must stop blaming the "consumer" fleeing from religion. Rather, we must revisit how religious people are representing religious virtues and how our religious leadership is honestly articulating twenty-first century religion as compelling, relevant, open, and transformational.

7.
WHAT'S THE SECRET TO JEWISH SURVIVAL?

Millennia of persecutions, expulsions, and massacres would surely mean the ruination of a nation, left as nothing but fragments of abstract his-tory. Yet, though many ancient peoples have disappeared from the face of the earth, with nothing but academic interest to keep their memories alive, what explains adequately the continued survival of the Jewish people other than calling it a miracle? Looking at the totality of Jewish suffering throughout the centuries lends itself to the theological conclusion that Divine intervention not only exists, but has actively led a role in shaping the world for the beleaguered Jewish people.

Acknowledging the presence of Divinity is a first step towards internalizing the remarkable journey of the Jewish nation and the wisdom that has contributed to making our existence possible despite every attempt to destroy our values and unique contributions to the humanity.

Though the human mind is incapable of understanding the exact reasons for Divine intervention, especially in relation to how Judaism has withstood so much baseless hatred, revulsion, and tragedy, I humbly submit five pieces of significant Jewish wisdom that helped make this survival, not only possible, but indicative of the indomitable Jewish spirit to thrive:

De-centralization – Since the destruction of the Second Temple, it became quickly apparent that individual Jewish communities (and indeed, individual Jews) could not be controlled. Religious hierarchies are imprudent, and trying to control something as complex and constantly evolving as the Jewish soul is folly. The trauma of losing the Temple ensured that empowerment over obedience was the new normal, and that inclusion over exclusion would allow communities to thrive. This has become increasingly true over the centuries.

Emphasis on Family and Community – The single greatest priority of Jewish intellectual life is the transmission of wisdom and a fidelity to a righteous way of life. By turning the home into the nucleus for incubating education and values, we enabled a unit for staying power. The self is not central and this mission requires humility to embrace the conviction that our legacy is through our youth which in turn gestates the survival of our community.

Outsider Status — When Abraham was mandated by God to be an ambassador for justice, he altered the course of Jewish existence. No longer could he blend into society and adopt the ways of social conformity. Although the Jewish people have often been forced to live as outsiders, this status was predestined through historical events. By being on the periphery of society, Jews have been in touch with other marginalized people and play a crucial role in making invisible people visible.

Trauma Memory — We cannot hide from the manifold traumas of the past, so we constantly have to remind ourselves to remain conscious of them and grow as a community. Remembering the Exodus from slavery, commemorating Tisha B'Av and destruction of the temples, observing *shiva* for a lost loved one, lighting a candle on Yom HaShoah, these are all emblems of Jewish pain. But in that pain, we join together. We heal together. We constantly remember together. Division ceases among the Jewish people and by holding onto the lingering pain, cultivates within us empathy for the countless many who are vulnerable.

Unique Societal Engagement — Jews remain distinct, but not separated from society. The model has not been complete isolation from society nor full integration assimilating into secular culture. We offer our own unique contributions to the world, while also learning from the society around us. Rambam taught that we must accept the truth from wherever we hear it. We engage with the world and the wisdom of our surrounding cultures but we bring our unique Jewish wisdom to it.

God gave Judaism the perspicacity to endure every hardship and tribulation. In the twenty-first century, each of these long-held values is challenged by the external and internal forces of assimilation, the breakdown of identity, and the corrosion of community; Jewish survival is being challenged in the process. There will always be those who attempt to control Jewish life in an autocratic manner, while others will try to act as insiders while throwing off their outsider identity. Some make Judaism about self-fulfillment rather than embracing transmission and family-based and community-based models. Thoughtlessly, some try to dismiss our historical consciousness and the responsibilities that come with it, while others unconditionally try to separate from the broader society altogether. There is no gain from losing one's identity caught by the zeitgeist of contemporary society, nor is it virtuous to expel oneself from the broader triumphs that secular society has afforded all people.

In the post-modern tumult that is contemporary society, there are so many different forms of Jewish wisdom that a person can embrace. Each of us has the faculties to choose from them, to discern their strengths and weaknesses. But one's voice can't simply be synonymous with any other American faction. For Jews in the United States, we're embedded within American culture and we can be proud of that. But we also must possess the consciousness that rises above the din of needless and pointless pabulum. It is our obligation to raise the discourse, applying our guiding Jewish principles to lead the way.

This is the secret of Jewish success, and always has been.

THEOLOGY

1.
Help! I Am Becoming a Panentheist: An Open Letter to Rav Kook

Rebbe, again and again, I pine for greater understanding of your metaphysical teachings. While I try to understand your seraphic cosmology, I desperately need assistance. Once again, I am deeply persuaded by your ideas and, yet, I feel stuck. I need your guidance.

It is clear that you are not a pantheist (equating the world with God) but rather striving for a panentheism (God is the world but also indomitably beyond, literally embracing that "all" is "in" "God"). God is in the world and the world is in God. As I also embrace this theology, I now see God as the only Being, the only Reality, the only true empyrean Existence (*ain od milvado*) in the *ein sof*—this world and the world beyond. The ethereal veiled Presence is everywhere; the diaphanous inner force hidden within everything. The interconnected relationship between everything is infused with the spark of God; a monistic reality.

Thankfully, I also have no inclinations toward pantheism where we lose God. Our goal is to recover God in infinite expansiveness. Our service through the physical—*avodah b'gashmiut*—discovers that the Divine Presence is truly pervasive, a ubiquitous single organism, one great living Being. Separation, a mere illusion, begins to fall away as we desperately cling to the immaculate scent of your immanence and transcendence.

I have more firmly approached the panentheistic leanings you share. You suggest a demanding ontology, one that I wrestle with intellectually and emotionally: "All existents are nothing other than tiny sparks in the light of that supernal reality" (*Orot HaKodesh* I, 214). I am challenged by the existential quest: "It is the unification of all moral claims which enter the heart of every creature, which embrace all human communities and unite all worlds" (*ibid.*, 11-12). And your intense epistemology suggests that it is not only in all being but "in every subject of study, there is a spark of the general light which is manifest in all existence" (*Orot HaTorah* III, 18).

When I study your texts, I am awed. Your words are beautiful, your thoughts inspired from the gossamer whispers of the Divine. But I am, on some level, afraid to invest more deeply. My questions are manifold: How can we handle the moral burden of seeing God everywhere and in everything? If I am obligated to Jews of every persuasion and every type of human, how can I ever pause from my service? If an animal and a plant participate in "Being," how can I, in any way, be involved in preventing their harm? If there is the spark of truth everywhere, how can I ever feel at all stable with what I know?

My rationalist side gives me comfort that there are limits and boundaries to my commitments and to God's light, but this mystical dimension shows that we are indeed immersed within Divinity and must break free from the illusions which give us structure; comfortable vanity? Is kenosis and radical self-emptying part of our goal? If God's infinity includes the finite as well and Divinity's eternal essence is complemented by a responsive dimension, where will embracing the Hegelian dialectical historical panentheism lead us next?

If nature is a part of Divinity then our natural morality is completely binding upon us. The force of intuition and conscience is enormous. How can we remain rationally grounded if we're fervently committed to seeing your Presence everywhere? How much can we allow the external voice of God codified be influenced by the Voice within? Further, I am so committed to the notion *tzimtzum*—the notion of space created for human freedom—and I am so emotionally committed to a personal God. I am afraid of where radical pervasiveness, inspired by your philosophy, will lead me. How are we to root, epistemically, any commitment to the identity of the non-divine? How are we to maintain a constant awareness of the radical Presence infused in all consciousness?

The burden of the Jewish soul is to comprehend its vast cosmic potential of the universe, within the limited realm of this temporal world. How can we reconcile this great disparity? Your words, clear and lucid, help guide me in my own journey towards ultimate understanding. But how do we break through our inhibitions to truly understand more deeply? Our partners in this journey are unconsciously everywhere yet consciously nowhere. The desire to know and to give so greatly exceeds our capacity for fruitful actualization and we must live within this painful paradox. If we tap into the All, can we receive help from above to achieve the near impossible?

You shared that "all human perception and knowledge... is laden with obscurity and error (*Orot Hakodesh I*, 11-12) and my humble conceptions are certainly included. Please help, Rebbe! We named our son "Kook" in order that fragments of your *gilgul* might be incarnate within him, but he is yet to speak.

I am scared. I am ready!

With deep admiration and love,
Your student desperately searching within and beyond,

Shmuly

2.
WHY WAS THE TORAH REVEALED OUTSIDE OF ISRAEL?

The question itself leaves us perplexed and humbled. Ostensibly, the situation is backward. If Israel is the Holy Land as described in the hallowed words of the Torah, why would the Holy Word itself not be revealed at the pinnacle historical moment: the arrival of the Israelites into the prophetic Promised Land? Wouldn't the fate and destiny of the Israelites be derived from happenings in their ancestral spiritual

One might suggest that the inhospitable desert was a training ground—a testing platform—to prepare the Jewish people for the rigors they were about to accept. Likewise, at a more basic level, it was used to confirm and reassure that they were indeed worthy to take up the sacred mantle of Torah law. One might suggest that, in addition to enduring the harsh terrain of the perilous desert, they needed to be free of the harsh cultural influences they absorbed while in Egypt and that they would encounter again in the Land. This new lifestyle and perspective — radical in scope, intimate in nature — would surely have been appropriate to inculcate once in the Promised Land.

What, then, is the ontological reason for this perplexing situation? Perhaps, we are learning that Torah is, at its core, more universalistic than particularistic, where it's transmission and internalization is inherently valid to all peoples. Or perhaps, the giving of Torah to Moses on Mt. Sinai was a gift to the last generation of Hebrew slaves, contingent upon accepting that their plight in Egypt is truly at an end, while still accepting that leaving Egypt was a traumatic experience; before this generation ceded its authority to the next one, it was vital that they all could joyfully accept Torah and the next generation of Israelites could then adopt this holy writ fulfilling the legacy within the borders of their ancestral home.

I'd like to suggest three additional perspectives. The first is based on a *midrash* that shares a profound Jewish teaching on pluralism:

Why was the Torah not given in the land of Israel?...To avoid causing dissension among the tribes. Else one might have said: 'In my territory the Torah was given.' And the other might have said: 'In my territory the Torah was given.' Therefore, the Torah was given in the desert, publicly and openly, in a place belonging to no one. To three things the Torah is likened: to the desert, to fire, and to water. This is to tell you that just as these three things are free to all who come into the world, so also are the words of the Torah free to all who come into the world (*Mekhilta B'Chodesh* 5).

To that point, no one faction of Judaism—a sad phrase to articulate in itself—can ever own the entirety of Torah. By revealing the Torah in an ownerless zone, no one can ever claim that they are the true inheritors and authorities. The Torah is revealed in the desert to teach us that we all are equal owners and guardians of the tradition.

An another approach is to consider the relationship between religious institutions and state, and the corresponding role of religion and broad sovereignty. Consequently, the Torah is revealed in the diaspora to teach that Judaism transcends statehood, sovereignty, or even a physical land to survive. The last two thousand years proves that. It can be understood then that revelation outside of Israel disseminates the deeply powerful pull of Judaism's intellectual breadth and fortitude in the face of endless persecution. The humble person of Jewish faith knows that their ancestral rights are not bound to the whims of governments and feckless empires, but by a contract that extends into the heavens and beyond. It is clear that Torah can, and must, exist separately from the flawed sovereignty of humanity; Torah has the ultimate power to inspire and educate, but not control or dictate.

Rabbi David Hartman shared a thought-provoking analysis on this view:

I give preference to the *midrashim* that imply that the covenant was made in the desert to teach the community that Judaism as a way of life was not exclusively a function of political sovereignty. We were born as a people within the desert in order to understand that the land must always be perceived as an instrumental and never as an absolute value. The memory that the covenant was made in the desert prevents us from falling victim to the idolatry of state power (*A Living Covenant*, 282).

Lastly, we can take a *mussar* approach to understand our question. Though we are "Chosen People," we are not superior to any other race or creed. We are placed upon this Earth to be symbols for justice and peace. The Torah could have been revealed nowhere else but outside the borders of the Holy Land, in the humble desert.

This was a deliberate choice, a pedagogical tool for the Jewish people: we are to walk in this same humility so that we do not force change upon others by way of sword.

Rabbi Yerucham Levovitz wrote:

Why was the Torah given in the wilderness at Mount Sinai and not in the calm and peacefulness of Israel? This is to teach us that true peace of mind doesn't come from physical comforts but from an awareness of one's ultimate life goals. When you focus on this, you are constantly traveling toward your goal and will never be overly disturbed or broken.

Indeed, had the Torah been revealed within the beautiful calm land of our destiny, we would have credited the external land for our inner peace. Rather than being a marker for any particular group, we needed to learn that peace is achieved internally. The Torah transforms our inner being and that can even happen in the chaotic barren desert.

Ultimately, we may never know the true reason why the Torah was given outside of Israel. The notion of a heavenly presence coming down to Earth, goes beyond our temporal understanding. What we can discern from our sages, however, is that there are manifold meanings in such a divine action and that each has its own relevance. As we yearn to seek the truth of the universe, we can look back to our ancestors and see what they went through to accept the words of Torah into their minds, their souls, their hearts. It is our task to see that their holy journey continues, made relevant for eons to come.

3.
Was Revelation a Divine Compromise?

From the opening book of the Torah, it seems God is continually disappointed with humanity. These moral disappointments, imbued with the heavenly spark, almost never live up to the Divine expectation. From the expulsion of Eden to Cain killing his brother Abel, the failings of the generation of the flood, and the necessary dispersion at Babel, humans fail repeatedly. Relying upon reason, conscience, and intuition should have been enough, but God foresaw that there must be an intervention to reinforce what humans already know via their natural morality. Thus, revelation.

But this was a dangerous task. Creating an authoritative mandate inevitability leads to rebellion, as is the human condition known from the first recorded human error (the eating of the fruit from the Tree of Knowledge). So, with this in mind, God makes a compromise by revealing to humans what they should already know (through learning, reflection, character development, and meditation).

The rabbis of the Talmud were explicit that the Torah was to reinforce what people could have learned from intuition and experience. For it is written: "If we had not received the Torah we would have learned modesty from watching a cat, honesty from the ant, and fidelity from the dove" (*Eruvin* 100b). There were, of course, the select few who understood the holy and true path before the rest of humanity. In the Abrahamic traditions, we call these learned few the Patriarchs, and indeed, the rabbis taught that the patriarchs already knew the Torah on their own without the need for revelation. "Abraham our Father fulfilled the entire Torah before it was given, even the laws of the Sabbath food preparation on a festival" (*Yoma* 28b). In a related explication of this thought centuries later, Rabbi Levi Yitzchok of Berditchev—the Kedushat Levi—explained that the Patriarchs knew the Torah intimately through their limbs: "248 positive commandments of the Torah parallel our 248 spiritual limbs; the Torah's 265 prohibitions are parallel to our 365 spiritual sinews" (*Kedushat Purim* #1). It is through the corporeality of the body—mind and experience—that we can already know Torah without external revelation.

The medieval Jewish philosophers—such as Maimonides and Saadya Gaon—were also clear that the dual entities reason and revelation do not contradict each other. Humans were not properly reaching the moral level God expected they would through reason and so Divine mercy provided for an adapted plan: thunderbolts, lightning and the direct word of God. Here, the Kedushat Levi taught that God is "clothed" at Sinai (as compared to being "unclothed" at the miracles of the Red Sea) teaching that revelation is more about deep intellectual and spiritual comprehension of values than about Divine connection (*Kedushat Levi, Parshat Yitro*).

To demonstrate another specific example of how human failure leads to the concession of revelation, Rabbi Obadiah ben Jacob Sforno argued that the laws of *kashrut* were given because of the sin of the Golden Calf (*Parshat Shemini*). These stipulations weren't part of the original plan but were revealed later to reconcile the Divine-human relationship after another colossal human failure.

Further, it may not be ideal that revelation happens to one people in particular. God had attempted to form more universal covenants through Noah and Abraham, though these didn't work to sustain moral commitment. Thus, God narrowed revelation down to one people, which is clearly not ideal for the God of all people and all Creation.

Only a moment after revelation, there is confusion of agreement on interpretation and truth gets fragmented. We always have access to truth within, but now we are confused being committed to a system of revelation that has imperfect transmission. It is far from ideal to have historical revelation compete with the revelation of now. We are stuck with this tension and must embrace both. This allows the revelation of the past and revelation of now to refine one another. The Hasidic masters conveyed to us that there are sparks of light and truth, however fragmented and garbed, to be found everywhere. That discovered light hidden within creation must penetrate our minds and souls.

Rav Kook taught that to silence our conscience is to destroy our fear of heaven, which is crucial for religious life. And, to be sure, the threat today in religious life is that we too often fail to develop our intrinsic, God-given capacities: reason, intuition, and conscience; we blindly obey historical revelation or the version that today's authorities highlight). Our first priority must be the innate Divine revelation—to guard and cultivate the holiness of our inner world—and the complimentary revelation reinforces and guides us toward particulars.

We should be grateful that a Divine concession was made to reinforce the just and holy path that is all too easily elusive without revelation.

The religious person is committed to revelation of Sinai and to the God-given truth within. For the word of God to be living, it must be alive in us, through our minds and our souls. We now live with a more complicated and less ideal world as we are filled with both consciousness of revelation and reason. In a post-Holocaust world, we must accept the standard that we expect for others; namely, that one can never again silence common moral intuition and human conscience in the name of obedience to authority, no matter who is being obeyed. To be religious means having the courage to walk in the ways of God transcending the vagaries of human authorities that block our own intellectual and spiritual responsibilities.

4.
AN OPEN LETTER TO BARUCH SPINOZA

I feel compelled to apologize to you.

Those of us who have remained religiously committed centuries after your life have all too often failed to investigate our creed with adequate rigor. We have replaced inquiry with exclusivity. Rather than courageously interrogating and boldly inquiring of the most perplexing questions of the universe, we have alienated—all too often—those who have come to conclusions outside our conformed norms.

We will never meet. While we would disagree (perhaps) on many matters, I'd like to think we'd enjoy each other's company. You were a bold pioneer ushering in Enlightenment and suffered for your intellectual authenticity. Excommunication from your Portuguese-Sephardic community when you were only a 23-year-old man must have been traumatic. In my time, being excommunicated is irrelevant for the majority of us, but in the seventeenth century, you had no real precedent. You had nowhere to go.

Israeli Prime Minister David Ben-Gurion (yes, how foreign a concept of a national state founded on the notion of Jewish self-determination!) asked the Chief Rabbi of the Portuguese-Spanish community six decades ago to lift your *cherem* (excommunication). He was unwilling. My revered teacher Rabbi Nathan Lopes Cardozo asked the current Chief Rabbi this year to lift the ban. He was unwilling. One day, your ideas will, God willing, be understood and your legacy vindicated. Indeed, rather than shunning you, we should be thanking you. Referring to your scholarship, a great scholar in our time, Rabbi Cardozo, wrote:

I love heresy because it forces us to rethink our religious beliefs. We owe nearly all of our knowledge not to those who have agreed but to those who have differed... I consider him a secular *tzaddik*. He lived by his noble ideas, was dedicated to simplicity, and showed the most remarkable virtuous characteristics... He surely helped us to think more maturely about God, human nature, happiness, and the society in which we live.

If I believe your ideas did harm to Judaism, I believe the proclamation for your banishment did more. Those who don't understand the subtle complexities of your ideas ban them simply for being foreign and threatening.

But these individuals are spiritually xenophobic. Your philosophy must, at the least, be understood. For doesn't Judaism thrive most amidst an open marketplace of ideas where critiques, protests, and counterpoints are not only to be welcomed but encouraged? Is not this the source of our intellectual sustenance? The ban on you has, for centuries, represented fear. And Judaism must embrace a bold and fearless journey forward.

Judaism shuns clinging to dogmas and the notions of religious exclusivity. Our normative practices reflect the intellectual ideals we hold dear. We must make clear, then, that the precepts of Torah embrace autonomy, open-thinking, hermeneutical diversity, and engaging with ideas that may be outside the comfortable framework that is all too prevalent in contemporary Jewish thought. Thus, defending you is defending the essence of Judaism itself.

May your *neshama* have an *aliyah*,

Shmuly

5.
DEVELOPING A SECOND HALAKHAH

I'd like to believe that the immutable beauty of Jewish law is a sacrosanct thing, one that everybody can accept with absolute certainty. Any why not? Hasn't this system kept the Jewish people rooted with ethical and spiritual priorities, guiding us throughout the millennia as we've been scattered throughout the precarious diaspora? *Halakhah* has always been a unique and complex process (legally and socially).

As the Orthodox community remains committed to these norms and to this discourse, other streams of Judaism continue to ebb away from the righteous rigor that Jewish law is meant to instill. Though it remains the guiding light of those who are (and deliberately choose to be) observant, there is the sad reality that for the vast majority of the Jewish people, the wonders of *halakhah* remain irrelevant.

Rabbi Yitz Greenberg, in an essay written in 1967, identified this divide well:

> Today, when the bulk of the Jewish people is alienated from the *halakhah* by lack of knowledge or by ideals which appear in their eyes to be superior to the *halakhah*, it seems to some that the *halakhists* becoming the way of a sect and that some new vehicle of Jewish religion must be in the making. Others who know its power and its beauty believe that the *halakhah* can reclaim the connection to the entire Jewish people by embracing all of life and by taking up and giving meaning to both sides of the dialectical tensions which affect all Jews.

In the modern realities we live in, I propose a radical solution fitting for our unique time. Judaism is in need of a second *halakhah*, one that is streamlined and elemental yet as meticulous as the *halakhah* we have known for generations. This second *halakhah* is meant to be a broad paradigm that all of the Jewish people can turn to and share. It is not meant to supersede the original *halakhah*, but only act as a supplement to the first.

Rav Soloveitchik, drawing from *midrashic* literature of the opening chapters of Genesis, wrote about the existence of two beings named Adam: Adam 1 and Adam 2. The first being named Adam— grand, noble, and majestic—is the basis for all humanity as we know it today. The second Adam is humble with a limited purpose

This existential condition is the representation of the need for two *halakhot*: a traditional *halakhah* that keeps us rooted and humble and a second *halakhah*, to be developed, is the noble enterprise of the entire Jewish people in its full grandeur. As Jews, we live with paradox, with multiple selves.

We cannot bridge the Divine and temporal together if we lack a shared vernacular. One segment seems to have lost the big picture stuck in minutiae while the other segment seems to be lost with the whims of the time without strong enough anchors. The Orthodox have to gain because it once again brings them to relevance within the broader Jewish people. The more liberal Jewish communities have to gain because there is a desperate need for a rooted discourse. There is not merely a value of "protecting strangers," for example, but detailed *halakhah* to be developed around our moral imperatives. What would a new rigorous model of ethical *kashrut* look like? What rules would a new model of Shabbat include? How about a creative model of *taharat mishpacha* (bringing purity into marital relationships)? *Clal Yisrael*, as a collective, gains the most from this new model since we are in desperate need of ensuring the survival of one people with some kind of sustained values and discourse. Our spiritual liberation, from our own intellectual narrowness, is bound up together.

Just as modern observant Jews have the experience of translating ancient Jewish wisdom into a secular language of public policy, so too we can build another intellectual bridge for the sake of peoplehood and what our people could produce together. This was attempted with *mishpat ivri* but it failed. In the end, the Orthodox wanted *halakhah* to rule the state and the secular wanted the state to be secular. There was no middle ground to meet around Jewish values. We must, humbly but boldly, try again.

So let's demonstrate now that a *halakhah* with branching paths is the new template for the Jewish people. In the first *halakhah*, we may have to look at twenty *respona* to properly permit a matter of certain interest. In the second, invoking *tzelem Elokim* (human dignity) may be enough. Yet, the results will be the same. Although there is now an alternative path, they each share the same end while simultaneously utilizing the same language without jeopardizing the integrity of either process. Where there are differences, we will embrace *makhloket l'shem* shamayim (argument for the sake of heaven) but remain in conversation together. Together we can strive for a unity that honors diversity. We can hold our absolutes and make room for others' absolutes.

Neither system of *halakhah* will demand that the other side act differently but will merely provide a similar language for all sides to learn together with unpredictable results. Neither side compromises their integrity but merely learns a new form of expansive engagement. The liberal Jew will seek a more rigorous and sustained Jewish commitment. The Orthodox Jew will maintain their full commitment to *halakhah* 1 but will also be challenged and broadened by relationships and perspectives from the encounter with *halakhah* 2.

Both sides will feel uncomfortable in a humbling and productive process of growth. This will not work for individuals from two extremes (one which claims they hold the sole truth and there is no truth beyond theirs nor for those who claim that Judaism cannot dictate our behavioral norms in any fashion at all). *Halakhah* 2 will have concrete norms but not so detailed and divisive as *halakhah* has become today. Each individual can't open opt out because they feel alienated from the existing model. Rather they can feel compelled to take responsibility for developing an authentic model that works for them.

There are many unanswered questions here and I am not the one to answer them. The process must develop with a lot of different participation and leadership.

This is no simple endeavor and we should not be so naïve to assume everyone will be on board nor should be so naïve to assume that these two systems will be more similar than different. But the alternative is to continue to point fingers and stubbornly throw our hands up in the name of fidelity to the epistemological structures we inherited. We must leave those who perpetually bring cynical energy to pluralism on the sidelines for now. Compromise is the great *mitzvah* that our people has failed to yet achieve (*Sanhedrin* 6b). Bridging our values and discourses is more crucial than ever before to ensure we can learn from one another and build synergy around the meta-goals of the Jewish people: to repair the world in partnered covenant with God.

6.
The Rebbe of Gur & the Power of Now

Can we learn to listen to this moment, and to the new moments as the unfold before our consciousness?

Being attuned to the moment is not easy. Even Moshe, Judaism's greatest prophet and leader, struggled with this. Maimonides explained that: "Moshe didn't see the presence of God at the burning bush right away, because he hadn't prepared his heart for prophecy" (Commentary on Exodus 3:2). The task, then, is to prepare ourselves for the radical possibility of every moment, or we will miss them. Indeed, we have to wonder just how much we're missing each day. Martin Buber, citing a Yom Kippur sermon from the Rebbe of Gur, recounts the wise, guiding words of the Rebbe:

The present, this "now," which is the moment during which we are speaking, did not exist when the world was created and will also never return. The present "now" was preceded by another "now" and will be followed by another "now." Each "now" has its own unique divine task (*Or HaGanuz*, 457-458).

To achieve such a lofty goal, we should not be slaves to the past. We cannot replay our actions over and over again and expect different results. Rather, we continue to learn and evolve as people, our souls becoming more experienced with the ways of the world; with every mistake, we surely must learn something. Holding onto the subtle, yet precious, moments can be increasingly challenging for individuals committed to tradition and to relying deeply on past rituals, ideas, memories. But the religious person learns to balance listening to the past while continuing to live in the moment.

We cannot look only backward and forward. We need to be broad and look outward as well. For this reason, Jewish law requires that there are windows in the synagogue:

One should only pray in a house which has windows, as it says, 'And Daniel would enter his house, where there were open windows in his upper chamber facing Jerusalem; three times a day he would kneel and pray' (*Berachot* 34b, quoting Daniel 6:11).

Based on this requirement, Rav Kook wrote:

Prayer is an intensely introspective activity, but it should not lead us to belittle the value of being part of the world around us. If meditation and private prayer lead us to withdraw from the outside world, then we have missed prayer's ultimate goal. The full import of prayer cannot be properly realized by those secluded in a monastery, cut off from the world. Prayer should inspire us to take action for just and worthy causes (*Ein Eyah vol. I* on *Berachot* 34b, 5:124).

Maimonides explained, even more strongly, that the greatest evils come from the spiritually blind, and if we don't open our eyes in the world, intellectually and spiritually, that we will actually cause great harm to others (*Guide for the Perplexed*, 3:11).

Professor Michael Fishbane, a theologian from the University of Chicago, beautifully explains the imperative of the moment:

Perhaps this: already with the opening of eyes, the hearing of ears, and the tactility of the body—already from such inadvertent moments the world imposes itself on us. It is always already there for me, just as I become there for it. There is no gap to be crossed (between the cognizing ego and the world): there is miraculously an immediate, primordial thereness of reality. Already from the first, and with every act of sensation, the world is "there" as a field of phenomenality, as a world of claims imposing themselves with an ever-present and evident presence. These claims put one under a primary obligation: one can respond or not respond; heal or destroy; attend or neglect; consume or build up. We have that choice (*Sacred Attunement*, 192).

In the twenty-first century, we have more distractions than ever preventing us from cultivating the spiritual art of focus to ensure we climb to the heights of our potential. The rabbis teach that one who pauses to enjoy nature flippantly while attempting to focus on higher spiritual matters "bears guilt upon their soul" (*Pirkei Avot* 3:9). "Stopping to smell the roses" is not always the best prescription for a spiritually present life.

Perhaps the most profound statement that our forefathers give in the Torah is *Hineini: Here I Am*. No matter what comes before us, we should strive to be present to that which is in front of us, and be appreciative of the moment, ready to take action, and always seeking the most important spiritual response to any problem we encounter. The theological model to emulate, thus, is the *Shekhinah* (the Divine Presence) as we strive to be entirely in the moment. It is our obligation to follow the *halakhic* model of *mitzvot tzrichot kavannah*—commandments that require presence and concentration; we emulate the Divine when we throw our full selves into our greatest life commitments.

We have a real choice to respond to the call of the moment. Ignoring it is an option, though one we should be loath to take. The great sage Hillel famously taught, "If not now, when?" There is no time like the now to embrace life and its sacred opportunities. Hillel also suggested that the Sabbath is not the sole time where we fine-tune our spiritual presence. Rather: *Baruch Hashem yom yom*—our holy tasks are a daily endeavor (*Beitzah* 16).

There is no time like now to start living in the now.

Indeed, it is all we have.

LEADERSHIP

1.
Rabbi Yitz Greenberg's "Sage Advice"

Every culture and faith tradition has its source of inspirational nuggets of eternal wisdom. In Daoism, there is the Dao De Jing; the Mormon canon has its Doctrines & Covenants; Islam has the *hadith*. Even the United States has *Poor Richard's Almanack* to look to for pithy sayings of mighty consequence. The Jewish tradition has countless anecdotes of imparted wisdom that guide countless people to navigate the world ethically and with purpose. Outside of biblical sources, the most succinct collection of sayings and parables is *Pirkei Avot*—the Ethics of the Fathers—a remarkably dense tome whose brevity and judiciousness has inspired an incalculable number of leaders, scholars, and laypeople throughout centuries of Jewish history.

Pirkei Avot, in its rawest form, is a stew of biblical textual interpretation and criticism, precepts, hermeneutical and epistemological innovation, and a practical guide to operating in a philosophically complicated world. In its verses are some of the greatest debates ever recorded in human history. Certainly, the division between the House of Shammai and the House of Hillel resulted in truisms that still hold court in the imagination of people to this day! It is not an exaggeration to write that the sayings that resulted from these disputes between great figures of Jewish history expanded the consciousness of an entire civilization. These are the words that are etched on the vestibules of time and space, that are uttered on the lips from the youngest learner to the oldest pedagogue, that are placed in the forefront of the mind to stretch it into new vistas of possibility; to be sure, "as profound educators, the sages spoke and taught on their students' level" (106). These qualities speak to the timelessness of a work that is a product of its time.

And indeed, due to its centrality in shaping the ethical development of the ages, the deeper meaning *Pirkei Avot* has constantly evolved, "[unveiling] a new level of revelation" with each successive generation (*xxviii*). Significant Jewish thinkers over the centuries, from Rav Shimshon Raphael Hirsch, to Rav Yehudah Aryeh Leib Alter (Sfat Emet), to Rav Yehudah Loew ben Bezalel (Maharal), have contributed their own interpretation of what the words of the early Jewish sages meant and will mean to contemporary adherents. And so it continues today…

Rabbi Dr. Irving (Yitz) Greenberg is the most significant Jewish voice in our time. His years of service in the rabbinate, as an organizational leader, as an author, and as an activist has allowed for great strides in promoting Jewish values across the spectrum of other religious traditions and cultures. Rav Yitz builds bridges within the Jewish community, builds bridges between faiths, and builds bridges between tradition and modernity. He has not only been the scholar that has facilitated the relevancy of modern Judaism but has been the leader who has engaged in building and nurturing a vibrant Jewish institutional landscape.

It gave me such a thrill when I saw that Rabbi Greenberg published a new commentary of *Pirkei Avot* titled *Sage Advice* (published by Maggid Books). It speaks to the capacity of the ancient sages to engender continuing relevance of their words and actions, presenting us with a singular resource that can (and must!) be interpreted again and again to continue to speak to our minds and souls.

This new tome is a perfect distillation of Rabbi Greenberg's dedication to synthesizing complex scholarship with accessibility. With a lucidity that is a hallmark of his writing, Rabbi Greenberg's commentary is as brilliantly thought-provoking as it is inspiring, taking each teaching of *Pirkei Avot* and breaking it down by section. Each passage gets its own analysis, and the critical reading of the text reveals the hidden wonders below the surface of the text. Rabbi Greenberg not only gives readers insight into the teachings but a view of the men behind the text. This extra step, beyond looking at the plain meaning of the passage, adds a layer of psychological verisimilitude to these ancient axioms. Readers aren't so removed from the words first recorded millennia ago. This is the secret weapon of *Sage Advice*: it's not a prescriptive book, but one that invites readers to join an epic journey that transcends the mundane into more supernal realms of understanding.

In these pages, Rabbi Greenberg adds another vital voice to a tradition that takes great care in discerning the transmission of the tradition from one generation to the next. This is surely a work that will take a valued place on many a Jewish bookshelf. Deservedly so. Readers who finish the book would be remiss to not simply start over again immediately, and allow these ancient words of wisdom to seep into their mind to lodge and become real forevermore. Rav Yitz and his "Sage Advice" are a treasure to the Jewish people.

2.
Learning Leadership From the Bible, Harvard, and a Chief Rabbi

To say that Rabbi Jonathan Sacks, the former Chief Rabbi of the United Kingdom, is one of the most prolific and powerful ambassadors for Judaism today is an understatement. When he speaks, people listen; when he writes, people read. This axiom is a testament to Rabbi Sacks' sheer intellectual contributions to contemporary religious thought, and not just for a Jewish audience. The underlying recipe of Rabbi Sacks' success as a thinker of the modern age is his accessibility: he writes for people of every creed, race, and type. And indeed, looking within the faith, his writing speaks to Jewish people of all denominations. He is a unifying religious scholar of the highest order.

Which is why I was so delighted with one of Rabbi Sacks' latest works: *Lessons in Leadership* (Maggid). Featuring a foreword by Professor Ronald Heifetz of the Harvard Kennedy School, *Lessons in Leadership* is a powerful, holistic treatise about approaches to Jewish power, how it's been applied throughout Jewish history, and what we can do to apply those lessons to the manifold problems that face humanity, let alone Judaism, today. It's a riveting read, and essential for those who look to take their leadership skills to a higher level.

Sacks found an ideal scholar in Professor Heifetz, to write the foreword to the book. In this way, Sacks allowed Heifetz to bring a certain secular, academic complement his own religiously-based ideas about the meaning of leadership. One of the first things Heifetz does is ask the reader the difference between authority and leadership and the consequences of comprehending such a critical distinction between the two:

The [Torah begins] to answer the central questions of authority and leadership: How can authority figures remain honest and trustworthy? How can we check the corrupting tendencies of centralized governance? How can people scarred by abusive authorities renew its ability to authorize and trust others? How did Moses, "the nursing father," succeed in transforming a slave-minded people—both deeply dependent on and deeply skeptical of authority—into a self-governing society? What principles of adaptability have enabled the Jewish community to survive and flourish over time? (*xviii*)

Certainly, Rabbi Sacks makes clear that he has been deeply influenced by Heifetz with regard to how he understands leadership in the Jewish tradition. A first point is on the difference between authority and leadership. Sacks identifies the prominent personage of Pharaoh as a figure who has the mantle of authority, but not leadership. In contrast, the more obscure figure of Nachson ben Aminadav, the first to enter the Red Sea that had not yet split, acted with no authority. In his action, he became one of the unsung heroes who comes to personify Jewish leadership. Sacks writes:

Judaism has tended to be critical of power. Kings had it and often abused it. Prophets had none, but their influence has lasted to this day. The Talmud tells that one *nasi* (head of the Jewish community), Rabban Gamliel, asserted the authority of his office in such a way has to humiliate his deputy, R. Yehoshua, and was deposed for so doing (*Berakhot* 27b). The *gedolei hador*, the great sages of the generation whose interpretation of Jewish law is usually followed, rarely — if ever — had formal authority. They simply emerge through common consent as the leading voices of their time. To a remarkable degree, Judaism is about leadership by influence, not about authority in virtue of formal office (xxiii-xxiv).

To be sure, Heifetz reminds readers that leadership is not some sort of zero-sum game. We can't abdicate responsibility for the actions of leaders who are not ready to take up the burden of responsibility themselves. (One might look at the the presidential primary circus of 2016 election as proof of the folly of finding gurus over serious and sensitive administrator.) We can't absolve ourselves of the sins of feckless leaders and expect everything to work as we want them to be. Indeed, as Heifetz writes:

[Too often], we look for the wrong kind of leadership. We call for someone with answers, decision, strength, and a map of the future, someone who knows where we ought to be going — in short, someone who can make hard problems simple... Instead of looking for saviors, we should be calling for leadership that will challenge us to face the problems for which there are no simple, painless solutions — the problems that require us to learn new ways (xv-xvi).

From there, Rabbi Sacks explains that there are three types of Torah: the Torah one learns from books, the Torah one learns from teachers, and the Torah one learns from life. He explains that his book was developed "[F]rom a life in active dialogue with Torah." And it shows. Heifetz explains the demands upon leadership:

Making progress on these problems demands not just someone who provides answers from on high, but changes in our attitudes, behavior, and values. To meet challenges such as these, we need a different idea of leadership and a new social contract that promotes our adaptive capacities rather than inappropriate expectations of authority. We need to re-conceive and revitalize our civic life and the meaning of leadership (*Leadership Without Easy Answers*, 2).

A second fundamental principle that Sacks learns from Heifetz is that leadership is not a personal trait or gift but a process one engages. Rabbi Sacks draws from many different leaders and their approaches. For Sacks, one of the greatest leaders of modern time was Rabbi Menachem Mendel Schneerson, the seventh rebbe of Chabad-Lubavitch. In describing the qualities that differentiate a good leader from a great leader, Sacks lays out his idiosyncratic but sincere criteria: "What I learned from him [the Lubavitcher Rebbe] was that a good leader creates followers. A great leader creates leaders. That is what the Rebbe did" (*xxvii*).

Such work is not easy. Rabbi Sacks explains that the relationship between a leader and follower is not an easy one. "A leader is one who challenges a follower. A follower is one who challenges a leader" (*xxvii*). One of the many factors that make this book work for a religious audience is that it is not a book on "how to succeed" in leadership. It's much more sophisticated than that. As Sacks writes: "[L]eadership is not only about what you achieve by it. It is what you become because of it" (*xxviii*). Sacks is as concerned, quite correctly, with our character and growth as he is with the consequences of our actions. And all who read his book will be much stronger leaders for it.

3.
STANDING TOGETHER IN THE ERA OF NATIONAL DIVISION: REVIEW OF "UNITED" BY SENATOR CORY BOOKER

In an interview with the *New York Times* on the eve of the 2016 release of his new book *United: Thoughts on Finding Common Ground and Advancing the Common Good* (Penguin Random House), Senator Cory Booker said something that was both revealing about his character and illuminating about his worldview. "I seek true stories that inspire..." the Junior Senator from New Jersey said, responding to a question about his favorite genres of literature. This could have been a buried statement. But for those involved in social justice activism, there is a lot to be discerned in this self-conscious statement, most noticeably its aspirational quality. In an economy of these simple words, Senator Booker laid out an expansive panorama of meaningful action, of social justice, of heart and soul. It was in these words that Senator Booker did something unique for a political tome. He not only laid out the thesis to his recently released book, he also revealed the underlying ethos of his profession: to inspire.

I think it would not be hyperbole to write that Cory Booker is one of the central figures for justice and forthrightness in America today. His history (as detailed in the book), from a football player in high school, to excelling at Stanford and Oxford before pursuing a degree from Yale Law School, all point to someone who could easily rest on the laurels of a distinguished resumé.

But this is not the case. This was not enough. Rather, throughout the book, Booker makes it plain, from an intellectual and social level, that being proactive and wading into the thicket of an unknown future is essential to the continuance of the traditions that bind us together. "Cynicism about America's current state of affairs," he writes, "is ultimately a form of surrender" (213).

The political story of Senator Cory Booker is one that is inherently American. It is the story of overcoming obstacles unfairly placed upon the stations of birth and race. Indeed, Booker eloquently writes early in the book that we should feel gratitude for the momentous opportunities that we are given by the singular nature of being Americans:

I've said many times of my generation that we drink deeply from wells of freedom and opportunity that we did not dig, that we eat from tables prepared for us by our ancestors, that we sit comfortably in the shade of trees that we did not cultivate. We stand on the shoulders of giants (9).

    I've always felt that as a politician, Booker has been one of the few shining stars on the scene. Every action he undertakes is as part of the community, instead of being outside of it. Though a Rhodes Scholar and graduate of the Ivy League, Booker has always been representative of a populace without those grand opportunities, whose struggles are more immediate to the streets than with the towers of knowledge: "I got my BA from Stanford, but I got my Ph.D from the streets of Newark" (a most telling passage). Instead of embarking on a corporate career, he moved to the economically distressed city of Newark, where he worked with poor residents on legal and housing issues. He later was elected to the Newark City Council in 1998. He then tangled with long-time mayor Sharpe James, a skillful politician in his own right but part of a more old-school machine mentality, and Booker lost his first mayoral contest in 2002. In a display of perspicacity that has continued, Booker recovered and won the mayoralty in 2006 and 2010. Then, after the passing of Frank Lautenberg in 2013, Booker won a special election to fill the vacant seat before winning election the following year to serve a full term in the World's Greatest Deliberative Body.

    Throughout his political career, as evidenced in the book and on his prodigious use of social media, Booker has demonstrated an ability not only to operate in a bipartisan fashion but also to speak out forcefully on issues near and dear to the heart of progressives. In 1992, while still a student at Stanford, Booker wrote Op-Ed for the Stanford Daily in which he decried his past homophobia (Senator Booker grew up in a strict, religious environment). He described his eventual realization that homophobic attitudes mirrored those of racism, and it made a profound impact on him; this was years before passage of the 1996 Defense of Marriage Act, signed by President Bill Clinton, that prevented federal recognition of gay marriage, even before states legalized it. Booker was decades ahead of the Democratic Party, indeed the majority of Americans, in recognized that the dignity of all people is sacrosanct.

    This is all part of personal evolution and the importance of moral development. And, to be sure, Booker calls upon his readers to act upon their highest values:

We make a grave mistake when we assume this spirit of connectedness is automatic or inevitable. It is not a birthright. A united country is an enduring struggle. It takes collective work and individual sacrifice. It is not enough to call on others or wait for a leader to emerge who will exalt our national values. I believe this is the question we face, as citizens of this nation: what will we do to affirm this most critical American virtue? (4).

To achieve such an end, Sen. Booker has worked in a pragmatic way across the aisle with Republicans to propose new ideas that may pass in a future Congress. In March 2015, Sen. Booker, Sen. Kirsten Gillibrand (D-NY), and Republican Sen. Rand Paul (R-KY) introduced a bill that would allow states to make medical marijuana policies without interference from the Federal government, and also allow doctors at Veterans Affairs hospitals to prescribe it to veterans. Since thirty-five states have some form of legal medical marijuana, this would create a much more stable legal situation. The bill was not acted upon, but a Senate Committee did vote in favor of a measure in May 2015 to allow Veterans Affairs physicians to sign recommendation forms for medical marijuana to veterans.

It's true that, at times, Booker has been criticized for being too cozy with big business and Republicans. As early as his days at Stanford University, Booker befriended many people who went on to become executives in Silicon Valley corporations, nationally known religious leaders, and leaders of the Republican party (indeed, New Jersey governor and failed 2016 presidential candidate Chris Christie is a long-time friend of Senator Booker). When Booker ran for the Senate, he was supported by Republican New York City mayor Michael Bloomberg. When he ran for re-election to the Senate in 2014, Wall Street firms gave Cory Booker nearly $1.88 million, more than any other Senator seeking office. In 2012, while campaigning for President Obama's reelection, Booker earned criticism from Democrats when he termed their attacks on Mitt Romney's wealth as "nauseating." But, as Booker writes: "Everything has a purpose… you can restore, recycle, redeem anything—or anybody" (207).

These partisan squabbles are, I feel, merely a byproduct of a natural tendency to pick tribes rather than unite to a common goal. If there is anything that Booker repeatedly returns to in United, it is that the myopia of contemporary politics leads citizens astray, and leaves them vulnerable to ignoring issues of tangible importance. "I believe that this broken system, which afflicts us all, will be repaired," writes Booker near the end of the book. To repeat an earlier point, what sets Senator Booker's work apart from that of similar political books is that it seeks to elevate discourse rather than bring down opponents of the opposite partisan persuasion.

This is a refreshing take, one that is truly worthy of study and contemplation. It makes us better citizens. Our nation deserves, and requires, more leaders in the vein of Senator Cory Booker. He is not a leader to merely "watch" but one to partner with and support.

4.
A Review of Zakheim's "Nehemiah: Statesman and Sage"

Today, many voices are yelling from the proverbial rooftops. Too often, though, they are of a demagogic variety, words spouted with the only intention to rile and to enrage rather than enlighten. The discourse between reasonable people, once so valued and vital to the continuance of civil society, has been replaced by an ever-increasing escalation of ad hominem attacks, character smears, and vacuous tête-à-têtes meant only to dull minds rather than uplift them. Contemporary society longs for wisdom, but in an era where prophecy no longer occurs, how can we reconcile the degradations of society with a positive message of moral change? Asked another way: What is the meaning of prophecy in a society that chooses to ignore its inner moral yearnings?

To move forward and seek the answers to improve communities around the world, it is optimal that we look back.

One of the recent guides to improving a collective vision of societal betterment is Rabbi Dr. Dov S. Zakheim's newly released, must-read book *Nehemiah: Statesman and Sage* (Maggid Publications). Nehemiah, whose contribution to biblical literature is less well-known when compared to his forbears Isaiah and Jeremiah, nonetheless is a figure worthy of study and rumination. Rabbi Dr. Zakheim, the former Under Secretary of Defense, places Nehemiah in a unique, dual context as an ethical philosopher and practical politician. In approaching the text, Zakheim appreciates both traditional sources (*midrashim* and commentators) and also critical academic scholarship. In his words, Zakheim laments that Nehemiah isn't given more status in Jewish appreciation: "It is a pity that even traditional Jews who are well versed in biblical lore have only a passing knowledge of this great man's life, times, and accomplishments" (6). The book, as such, is not a biography of the man, but an accessible, erudite work that allows readers to extrapolate the fifth century world (as Nehemiah saw it) and how we can apply those lessons in the twenty-first century.

Intertwining of religion and politics, as we know from our post-modern perch, is usually a hazardous combination. But during the days of Nehemiah and the Prophets, the expectation was that a society would choose a religion and weave it into civil life. How best to do that, however, was up to dispute. Interests of state—to keep peace or to make conquest—needed influential leaders. And those leaders needed strong voices in their decision-making process. The standard thought of hoary kings sending out men to die does not offer us much inspiration for us to go out into the world and make positive change. Thus, in the preface to his book, Zakheim writes that it was the great sage Nehemiah himself who helped motivate him toward government work and helped guide his moral deliberations:

I admired Nehemiah as a man who made a lasting mark both as a statesman and as a religious leader, one whose activities offered an enduring example for later generations to emulate. As I moved up the ranks of officialdom, Nehemiah continued to offer a compelling model of what leadership and religious commitment were all about (ix).

So then, it is an asset to readers that Zakheim understands both Torah and government and presents the life of Nehemiah as one motivated by the desire to see the betterment of the Jewish people while improving the broader society in which they lived. Nehemiah was both active in the Jewish rebuilding of Jerusalem during the Second Temple period as well as a governor of Persian Judea under Artaxerxes I of Persia (fifth century BCE). And many of those efforts have been misunderstood by later commentators and students of the Scripture. For though Nehemiah was a "man who revived in his demoralized people the sense of religious and national commitment," he also "struggled to establish a viable, pulsating, dynamic Jewish polity."

Zakheim describes why Nehemiah was such a pivotal figure in his time:

It was Nehemiah who successfully reconstructed Jerusalem's walls and provided for its security just over a half-century after the Temple was rebuilt. And it was Nehemiah who restored national pride and imposed a social and religious order based on tradition, justice, and decency (2).

Professor Martin Lockshin, a Bible scholar, writes about the prophet's activist zeal to protect the tradition:

Nehemiah, perhaps the more astute political pragmatist, tried to prevent future intermarriages, not to terminate existing ones. In other areas, Nehemiah took strident steps. He rebuked Jewish community leaders for allowing commerce in Jerusalem on the Sabbath. Once he won that battle and successfully closed

Jerusalem to commerce on the Sabbath, he chased away merchants who tried to circumvent the blue laws by setting up shop outside the city walls (Nehemiah 13:14-22)... The book of Ezra was written mostly in Aramaic, but Nehemiah's memoir, entirely in Hebrew, mentions how he railed against those who were raising children who could not speak proper Hebrew (Nehemiah 13:24).

    Rabbi Adin Steinsaltz, one of the great Torah sages of our time, has written about Nehemiah: "Not only was he a man of great spiritual and intellectual powers, but he was also a brilliant man of action" (*Biblical Images*, 208). That Nehemiah was a great man with flaws only cements his work, rather than diminish it. The legacy of Nehemiah remains complicated and the rabbis of the Talmud, for their part, had an ambivalence toward him. They reasoned that the basis for why he initially didn't have his own book in the Bible was due to his lack of humility and that he was too self-serving for his own causes (Sanhedrin 93b). Zakheim notes that: "Nehemiah's memoir was subsumed within the Book of Ezra; it was only in the Middle Ages... that Nehemiah was credited with his own book of Scripture" (2-3).

    For contemporary readers, the main takeaway from Zakheim's book is clear: We need more people like Nehemiah if we are to progress as a society. Too often we are consumed with the notion that personal flaws translate into weaknesses of leadership. Perfection isn't a virtue when lives are at stake. Even if there are qualms with certain facets of an individual's disposition or ethos, personal character development is a noble cause that all should strive for. Indeed, it is not mere actions that engender positive change, but the moral character demonstrated in the process. That's an inspiring requirement for religious as well as secular leadership.

5.
Bold Protest or Blind Faith?

The heroic figures of the Bible use their station to teach us that faith isn't about passivity, but protest. It is the primary role of the Jew to be an ambassador for justice. Our individual relationships with God should not merely comfort us, but rather, they are meant to be a challenge to us. Judaism is not to be an "opiate of the masses," as one of our co-religionists thought, but a holy challenge to our community to be more and to do more.

We can see this on display during the Torah portion (*parsha*) of *Vayeira* (Genesis 18:1–22:24) . At the beginning of the *parsha*, Abraham challenges God. For any other person, the notion that God would destroy the wicked cities of Sodom and Gomorrah would be a fait accompli. But our forefather Abraham was no ordinary person. He had the chutzpah to stand before the Creator of the world and say: "Will you stamp out the righteous along with the wicked?... It would be sacrilege for You to do such a thing, to bring death upon the righteous along with the wicked; so the righteous will be like the wicked. It would be sacrilege to You! Shall the Judge of all the earth not do justice?" (Genesis 18:23-25).

So then, how is it that this is the same person who, at the end of this *parsha*, blindly follows God during the *Akeidah*—the binding of Isaac. God said he would destroy the wicked and Abraham immediately rose to their defense. When God demands that Abraham kill his precious son, however, Abraham obeys without defiance. Where is our hero with the audacious *chutzpah*?

Ralbag (Gersonides) suggested that God never commanded the killing of Isaac. God is inherently good, but this command, by any moral account, would be evil. Rather, Ralbag proposed that Abraham misunderstood the command. Abraham was commanded to bring Isaac to the top of the mountain but never to kill him. Still, even if he misunderstood, why was Abraham so willing to go through with the deed?

I'd like to suggest that what Abraham misunderstood was God's response to the protest of Sodom and Gomorrah's destruction. Abraham protested and God, of course, proved himself right. Thus, Abraham mistakenly concluded that he should live by blind faith alone rather than with reason and conscience.

This is not what God asks of us. Abraham should have protested the binding of Isaac as forcefully as he asked to spare Sodom and Gomorrah. We are to struggle with our faith, not merely to submit to it.

Our challenge, then, is to develop a critical and moral reasoning capacity, to listen to the light of our conscience. Rav Kook had harsh words for those who misunderstood the Torah by trying to silence their conscience. He wrote:

The profound natural conscience's power and grandeur must be fortified within us as a spiritual basis for the potent radiance of the Torah. ...Whatever agrees with reason and our inborn sense of the fair must follow the course marked out by man's intuition and pure will. The Torah granted to Israel diffuses to us and to the world a brightness more luminous, pervasive and holy than that of natural reason and morality. Those who slight the elemental Divine appeal that re-echoes humanity's natural disposition and seek the supernal Torah light beyond the brilliance of the human soul, misconstrue the Torah (*Orot HaTorah*, 69-71).

Abraham was right to live by the faith of his inner light to challenge God. He misunderstood that result when he tried to live by blind faith and commit an act of potential evil. It is a vital lesson for all of us that an essential part of growing in Jewish wisdom is not simply learning texts and the ideas of the sages, but to enhance and beautify the truths that emerge from our own godly souls.

SOCIAL JUSTICE

1.
SEE THE INVISIBLE PEOPLE:
THE HIDDEN CRY OF OUR GENERATION

"Every generation has its own cry, sometimes open, sometimes hidden; sometimes the baby himself doesn't know that he's crying, and hence we have to try to be attentive to the hidden cries as well." – Rav Yehuda Amital, zt'l, Rosh Yeshiva Yeshivat Har Etzion and member of the Knesset.

Can you hear them?

Everywhere, there are invisible people with hidden cries. They are victims of deep injustices and violent oppression. They are the boys who wash our dishes at restaurants and the men who wash our cars. They are the girls who make our hotel beds and the women who serve in our homes. They are the slaves confined by our penal code and the objectified defined by sexual appetites. They are the homeless, spending their days in the shadow of our contempt and their nights in our parks of denial.

Theirs are the open cries reverberating within our souls and the loud cries of the streets. Theirs are the subterranean cries of those yearning for support and comfort.

Do you hear them?

We are in a precarious time. Years of recession and the rise of a new class of political and economic demagogues has cleaved our nation into haves and have-nots. Welfare—so demonized for the struggling family, the working single-mother, the recovering addict, the refugee—flows plentifully into the pockets of those who have sought to swindle and bankrupt our society. For too long, policies injurious to the vulnerable have proliferated and tragically become normal, leaving a significant void in the capacity for empathy development in the next generation. This generation's purpose is to rectify this gap, and fill it's chasm with love towards all of Creation. We must hear the voiceless, see the invisible.

For isn't it all too true that a person who lacks even the most basic of needs often wishes not to be seen, for any pretense of dependence on greater society is seen as capitulation? There is a deep shame that is felt when a person is at their lowest, without the means to make even the slightest inroads of improving their station of life. This engenders anger, which morphs into shame. And this shame is seen as all the more worse as it clouds the ability for people to reach out for help, to be visible to others that want to help them. It is a bitter cycle. When Nelson Mandela rose to become the first democratically elected President of South Africa, a country marred by a history of injustice the likes modern societies had so rarely experienced, he shared that "As we are liberated from our own fear, our presence automatically liberates others." It is our duty to take his admonition to heart. We need the courage to see and make seen the victims of injustice among us.

But these words are from another generation, and surely, haven't we learned much since then?

Will you hear them?

The great Hasidic master Maggid of Mezritch helped introduce the notion of *yesh me'ayin*—creation out of nothing. In his mystical ways, he taught that helping those who lurk in the shadows is akin to something coming into existence that previously did not exist, providing light to something that previously was unseen; for this is compared to the creation of the universe itself.

One of the primary goals of Jewish spiritual life is to see beyond the physical, to sanctify the unseen, to elevate matter to a higher plane. This is the meaning of the quote by Rav Amital that adorns this essay: that our task is to hear the unique cries of people who are often torn asunder from normal society, from normal time, from normal life; we need to uncover the hidden cries that call to us. In many ways, the cultivation of this ability to listen and respond is the central goal of religious living.

Without question, Jewish law demands not only that we see but that we be seen—*yireh, yai'raeh*— in Jerusalem on the festivals (*Chagigah* 2a). This law is not a relic. It is moral training for our eyes, our hearts; we are to be open and see those who are unseen. Connecting and supporting the unseen is not a distraction from tradition, but its actualization. Greater than lending money or giving *tzedakah* to a poor individual, the rabbis tell us, is providing partnership (*Shabbat* 63a). Seeing all people as equal goes far towards treating them with respect and dignity; we cannot discount those who are different.

Fortunately, we have been granted the abilities to help make visible those who society would deem invisible. We accomplish this by letting the vulnerable seek out succor they desperately need. We offer unconditional love, no judgement of status, only hope. For indeed, only hope and love can bring gleams of solace. Every time we encounter these people who dwell in the shadows, who are ignored and considered as the dregs of society, we must transcend our own pride, our own ego, and bend down to lend a proud, outstretched hand. Some of the most terrifying times in my own life have been when I didn't really feel like I existed; in these moments, I didn't feel acknowledged by the world, let alone appreciated or loved. These are times I often reflect on before beginning a mission to help those who are still left to wander the world without guidance and love.

But do we hear it?

I have been fortunate to have the support to get through those times. I know that I am not alone. In having had these feelings, neither am I alone in recognizing the crucial role played by friends and family members to remind me of my visibility and humanity. Our obligations in this life is to not forget the stranger that lurks out of our periphery. Let us be their friends, let us be their family members, and let us be their advocates. As Joni Mitchell sang: "Every picture has its shadows/And it has some source of light" Our charge is to join the invisible in solidarity and partnership: Let us help make their voices heard and their humanity seen.

Let us hear it.

2.
THE URGENT NEED FOR A LIVING WAGE

During every presidential election cycle, there comes with it additional pondering on the sort of nation we want to be. Are we a nation that believes in justice over inequality, of equal access over preferential treatment? Or are we a nation that ignores pressing social issues out of convenience, leaving those who are on the cusp of society—many through no fault of their own—to wallow through wave after wave of institutional roadblocks and bureaucratic recalcitrance. Though there is evidence to the contrary, I don't believe we are the type of country that shuns economic justice. As we enter further into the twenty-first century, new visions of how people make their way in the world will be tantamount to a social revolution.

Imagine, if you will for a moment, the plight of an unwed mother living in the South East side of Washington, DC. Abandoned by an abusive boyfriend, shunned from family and left to fend for herself and her child, Mother struggles to pay the bills. Her hourly income to support herself and her child should be around $30 to meet their most basic needs. Though she has a job to provide for her family, she is only paid the minimum wage in Washington, which, in 2016, is a little less than $10 per hour. That gap of nearly $20 means that despite all the hard work Mother puts in to care for her child, life is economically unsustainable.

But even beyond the metropolises that dot the United States, income inequality is stark and unrelenting; the cost of living is enormously high throughout the nation. Indeed, reducing the gap one earns and one needs to live is one of the most crucial moral issues that needs addressing in contemporary American society. Much of the problems that face the sustainable growth in our country has to do with the issue of fair wages and a reasonable income. Progress, while extremely slow, has been made. By January 2016, fourteen states modestly raised their minimum wage, yet the federal wage is still aggravatingly low for the majority of low-income workers, stuck at $7.25 an hour. The integrity of our sacred duty to ensure that all people are treated in a fair manner is at stake.

It is time for not only a higher minimum wage to be raised across the board, but for the introduction of living wage legislation so that *all* people have a chance to thrive and provide for themselves and their families.

While I am not an economist, let's take a look at some figures we can all understand: one working in New York City on the current minimum wage of $7.25 an hour will have a gross annual income between $12,000-$14,500, based on a projected model of a 35- to 40-hour work week. There are taxes involved—Social Security, income, state, and payroll for example—and monies deducted from other aspects of work. Even with a minimum wage at one place of employment, those who are economically vulnerable often have to work multiple jobs, with little time to devote to much else. Why should an individual, working long hours and within the confines of the law, be denied from thriving with the means they attain? Is that a just system worthy of the American dream?

The latent economic injustice of wage inequality is shattering. During the Great Recession, the American family lost nearly 40 percent of its wealth. Concurrently, as average families suffered, 95 percent of all new wealth generated was accumulated by the wealthiest 1 percent of the population. As an example: six members of the Walton family—descendants of Sam Walton, founder of Walmart—own more wealth than 41.5 percent of Americans, nearly the same amount of fifty million families combined. One member of the family had so much money tied up in fine art that she opened an art museum in Arkansas. At what point is accumulating more and more money obscene when employees of the company are making such small wages? Is it morally tolerable that the employee of a multi-billion dollar company is paid poverty-level wages?

Indeed, I don't buy the notion that raising the minimum wage, or even moving towards a living wage model, will negatively impact the amount of productivity that will be outputted back into the economy. To the contrary, the notion that lifting millions out of poverty with fair wages and a modicum security should be an aspiration for activists and employers alike. It is unjust to argue that one working all day every day should live in poverty. There is no theory that trumps the imperative for basic justice in a nation with record corporate profits. Furthermore, minimum wage workers tend to cluster in industries that cannot be outsourced or outright eliminated, so it is unlikely that a rise in minimum wage could curtail minimization of these jobs. With plentiful economic data, one significant study that researched the food industry found that raising the minimum wage did not result in employers trimming their workforce, and dozens of studies have confirmed these conclusion. But why is that?

In 2015, Nobel Prize winning economist and professor Paul Krugman, writing in the *New York Times*, commented that:

> ...[M]ost economists, myself included, assumed that raising the minimum wage would have a clear negative effect on employment. But they found, if anything, a positive effect... There's just no evidence that raising the minimum wage costs jobs, at least when the starting point is as low as it is in modern America. How can this be? There are several answers, but the most important is probably that the market for labor isn't like the market for, say, wheat, because workers are people. And because they're people, there are important benefits, even to the employer, from paying them more: better morale, lower turnover, increased productivity. These benefits largely offset the direct effect of higher labor costs, so that raising the minimum wage needn't cost jobs after all.

The fight for a more sustainable economic justice is not rooted in class warfare or a cynical ploy of avariciousness, but a positive step towards reducing the gap between those in opulent wealth and those barely above penury. Though countless people who are earning a low-income are working extraordinarily hard for their families, their hard work is not rewarded by a system that favors fairness and justice. Instead, there are interests that would prefer to stockpile their money than give it back to the people who have earned it. This cannot be the system we need to fight for. We need a social revolution, one that treats workers with respect and promises that they will be adequately compensated for their hard work.

A living wage is no longer a farfetched postulation from an obscure macroeconomic journal. It is part of the struggle for the American soul. It is a cause worthy of our support and one that will lift the spirits of millions of people, bringing a sense of equity back to a divided nation.

3.
Jewish Leaders Take A Stand Against The Death Penalty

In a petition initiated by Uri L'Tzedek, the Orthodox social justice movement, Jewish leaders across Jewish denominations expressed opposition to the use of the death penalty in America. As Jews, as citizens of a nation dedicated to liberty and justice, we believe that governments must protect the dignity and rights of every human being. The use of the death penalty in America fails to live up to this basic requirement.

Opposition to the overuse of capital punishment is embedded deep in the Jewish religious psyche. The rabbis taught that a court that puts others to death too often is deeply problematic. How often? Rabbi Eliezer ben Azariah says, "Every seventy years." Rabbi Tarfon and Rabbi Akiva said: "If we were in a court, no person would ever be executed" (*Makkot* 7a). While not categorically opposed to capital punishment, the rabbis saw the death penalty as so extreme a measure that they all but removed it from their system of justice. In contrast, our American system today lacks the highest safeguards to protect the lives of the innocent and uses capital punishment all too readily.

We do not naïvely believe that everyone on death row is completely innocent of any crime. Yet, too often, the wrong person is convicted for crimes they did not commit.

We all agree that a responsible government must have a strong, punitive justice system that maintains order and security. More harmful to our justice system than not catching the guilty, however, is punishing the innocent. Unfortunately, this happens too frequently. Owing to their socio-economic situation or lack of access to adequate legal resources, wrongly convicted people often have no real opportunity to respond to an overwhelming legal system that makes the proof of innocence difficult. The consequences of this system are not only fundamentally unjust but also produce racially disparate outcomes. Additionally, it is the tax payers themselves who are required to pay the exorbitant amounts to maintain death rows.

It is time to see the death penalty for what it is: not as justice gone awry, but a symptom of injustice as status quo:

You must rescue those taken off to death! (Proverbs 24:11)

There are six primary reasons for wrongful convictions:

Eyewitness misidentification — Some of the reasons for why eyewitnesses iden-tify the wrong person are not fixable, such as the fact that people are much worse at cross-racial identification, but there are many things that police can do when conducting line-ups that would decrease false identifications.

False confessions — A recent example of this is the case of the Central Park Five, in which four of the five then-teenagers confessed to raping and killing a woman in Central Park years ago, and recently were proven innocent through DNA testing.

Ineffective lawyering — Defense lawyers mess up, either because they just are not good lawyers or because they are so overburdened that it is impossible to do a thorough job on each case.

Police and prosecutorial misconduct — Examples of this include crime labs claiming that they had test results when no tests were actually performed, and prosecutors not providing exculpatory evidence. Unfortunately, punishment is rare.

Junk science — This applies both to methods that are not really science when empirically tested, and to legitimate science performed poorly.

Unreliable testimony — Witnesses, usually in jail, come forward claiming to have heard the suspect confess in order to get favorable treatment on their own cases.

How many prisoners are truly innocent? Experts have offered varying percentages in the last decades: Samuel R. Gross and Barbara O'Brien estimated "at least 2.3 percent"; Jon B. Gould and Richard A. Leo put it at 3 to 5 percent; James S. Liebman and his team placed their estimate at 7 percent; and the newest estimate, by John Roman and his team, places its estimate at 5 percent, except for sexual assault, for which the wrongful conviction rate may be as high as 15 percent.

Jewish law strongly upholds the principle that the innocent should be spared undue punishment. When God revealed to Abraham his plan to destroy Sodom and Gomorrah (Genesis 18:17-33), Abraham challenges God: "Will you also destroy the righteous with the wicked?" When God offers to spare the cities if there are fifty righteous people, Abraham solicits a response for the value of innocent life; eventually, God decides that if there are even ten righteous people, God will spare the cities. Abraham doesn't press further but one might presume that a city can't be destroyed if even one were innocent. Thus, from the time of Abraham, it was important that punishment should be reserved for the guilty, and against all odds to the contrary, the innocent should be spared.

Today, there are those who are dedicated to ensuring that the innocent do not languish in jail. The National Registry of Exonerations, a joint project of the University of Michigan Law School and the Center on Wrongful Convictions at Northwestern University School of Law, has now recorded 1,040 exonerations in less than a year of investigating data since 1989. The Registry highlights the need to scrutinize convictions—especially in the states with the most exonerations, such as Illinois and Texas—to ensure that they were honestly obtained and that the defendants had sufficient and competent defense.

Additionally, the Innocence Project, founded by Barry C. Scheck and Peter J. Neufeld of Yeshiva University's Benjamin N. Cardozo School of Law in 1992, is a group that utilizes DNA testing and other state of the art technology to establish the innocence of falsely-imprisoned inmates. The staff of lawyers and Cardozo clinic students, and allies in many states, has thus far exonerated 301 prisoners, who had served an average of nearly fourteen years (and eighteen of whom had been on death row), using DNA evidence. There are more than fifty Innocence Projects in the United States, under the umbrella of the Innocence Network. They need our support.

One case illustrates the great value of the Innocence Project for American society. In 1974, James Bain was convicted of raping a 9-year old boy in Florida. The primary evidence at the time revolved around the blood type of the semen on the victim's underwear. The jury believed the prosecution's claim that Bain's blood type (AB) was the same as that found on the scene, when in actuality the blood sample was blood group B. Once DNA evidence became available, Bain tried five times to get the Circuit Court to examine his case, but was rejected. Finally, after the Innocence Project became involved, DNA evidence was reexamined, confirming that Bain was not the rapist. James Bain was exonerated and released in December 2009, after serving thirty-five years for a crime he did not commit.

We need a justice system. But we also need a system of justice. We punish those who transgress the law, but ensure that the rights of the innocent are protected, that if a prisoner is found to be innocent, then that prisoner should be set free and given fair compensation. Former district attorney, Governor of California, and Supreme Court Chief Justice Earl Warren was well aware of the often coercive methods by which law enforcement obtained confessions and convictions, and how scrutiny needed to be applied to ensure that only the guilty were convicted and incarcerated. As he said: "Life and liberty can be as much endangered from illegal methods used to convict those thought to be criminals as from the actual criminals themselves."

This is nothing short of the championing of justice over inequity, and as a community, we must support their work. Jewish community leaders should call for an end to this cruel practice, but also for the beginning of a new paradigm of fair, equitable, and restorative justice.

4.
ZUCKERBERG & CLINTON:
A JEWISH PERSPECTIVE OF ALTRUISM

Altruism, as a construct, runs deep through the annals of religious philosophy. From a Christian perspective, altruism most commonly de-pends on the notion that human beings are, selflessly, to sacrifice comfort and well-being to give to another. This emerges from a theology where the Christian redeemer (divinity in human flesh) gives the ultimate sacrifice and thus serves as a model for emulation. Consider the heroic Mother Theresa who left her country, had no family, and served the poor in the streets in a foreign land. From a Jewish frame, giving to others is surely an imperative, but there is generally more emphasis on accommodating self-interest and the complexity of motives while doing so.

The Hebrew word for sacrifice is *korban* which comes from *karov*—to draw close. In sacrificing, we have a primary goal to come closer to the other or Other. Indeed, the Torah states: "You shall surely give him, and let your heart not feel bad when you give him..." (Deuteronomy 15:10). Our motives are not purely altruistic in the self-sacrificial sense of the word. Indeed, there is no virtue to lose or to feel bad after giving. This is reflected in other traditions as well. Aristotle in fact argued—correctly—that something would be wrong if we felt bad when we gave. Rather the virtuous person has their emotions and actions in sync and feels good when doing good and bad when doing bad. In the Talmud, the rabbis commented that one should: "Give tithes in order that you shall be enriched" (*Ta'anit* 9a). Gaining, as others gain, is a more sustainable win-win. Rabban Yochanan ben Zakkai argued that we seek atonement through acts of kindness (*Avot d'Rabbi Natan*, 11a). Our motive may be to fulfill the psychological need for purity and to remove guilt, but we help others in the process.

On a spiritual level, Rabbi Moshe Cordevero argued: "All souls are united, and each soul contains a part of all others" (*Tomer Devorah* 1:3). His student Rabbi Eliyahu de Vidas elaborated on this idea:

Even though your body's material substance separates you from your friend, the *nefesh*-soul of both of you is a spiritual entity and the tendency of the spirit is to make you cleave to your friend with unbroken unity. When your *nefesh*-soul—becomes aroused to love a friend, your friend's *nefesh*-soul will be equally aroused to love you in return until both of your souls are bound to form one single entity" (*Reishit Chochmah, Sha'ar Ha'Ahava*).

Imagine if we viewed the world in such a fashion: that investing in others is investing in ourselves. Ultimately, the sparks of our souls all return to the same fire. We are all different, but we are also one. We are loved by others because we show them love. We live in a community that is joyous and meaningful because we invest in it.

Historically, we see this precept through the life of Andrew Carnegie, who built an unprecedented steel empire in the late nineteenth century. When workers launched a strike for better pay and lower hours in 1892 at the Homestead steel plant, Carnegie backed a brutal crackdown that included crushing the union, causing loss of life. He later expressed regret over his actions. By the turn of the century, Carnegie publicly changed his attitude, and became the premier champion of philanthropy. By the time he passed, he had donated $350 million to charity, most notably building 2,500 public libraries and universities. Today, far more people are aware of Carnegie Hall than they are of the Homestead strike. The fact that he needed to rebuild his reputation and leave a positive legacy matters less than the contributions he has made that enriched so many. We need not judge others who give; neither the millionaires nor those who give on any level. "Man sees what is visible, but God sees into the heart" (I Samuel 16:7). What matters is most is that we foster a culture of giving, giving that builds a healthy and just society and helps those in need.

Let's look at a recent example of this altruistic spirit: The case of Facebook founder Mark Zuckerberg and his wife Priscilla Chan. They have donated millions of dollars to health care and education, including $100 million donated to Newark, New Jersey to improve the public school system. Zuckerberg dwarfed these contributions with a pledge in December 2015 to donate 99 percent of his Facebook stock (valued then at nearly $45 billion) to charity over the course of his lifetime. Zuckerberg, whose $6.2 billion stock gain in January 2016 bucked a downward stock slid and is now worth $47.6 billion. In keeping with other astute entrepreneurs such as Warren Buffett, however, Zuckerberg is not going to sell his stock and donate the cash, as he would then have to pay capital gains on the stock. Instead, he will donate up to 50 percent of his adjusted gross income (the maximum IRS limit for donations) by donating the stock itself when it gets to a high level, thereby maximizing the deduction and avoiding taxes. Meanwhile, charities that are given these stocks can then sell them without paying capital gains tax. Over the next several years, for example, Zuckerberg will donate no more than $1 billion annually; with this substantial amount, many will benefit. The fact that the philanthropist has tax benefits should be no grounds for critique.

Another paragon of altruistic giving is The Clinton Foundation. Founded by former President Bill Clinton shortly after leaving office in 2001, the credo of the Foundation is to combine the forces of governments, businesses and non-profit organizations to take on major problems facing the globe. The first, launched in 2002 to deal with the HIV/AIDS epidemic and now known as the Clinton Health Access Initiative, works to increase affordable access to health care internationally, including vaccines and treatments for malaria, tuberculosis, and other diseases. Many current initiatives focus on policies dealing with climate change as well as sustainable growth programs for Africa and Latin America, an American health program to combat obesity and common ailments, and international programs to promote education, equal rights, and health care for girls and women. While the Foundation has highlighted important areas for international co-operation, it also has kept the former President in the spotlight, assisted Hillary Clinton in her Presidential aspirations, and, presumably, set the stage in case their daughter Chelsea wishes to enter the political arena. Again, this heroic work should be applauded regardless of the fact that the Clintons gain in the process.

For those of us without access to billions, we are still able to do our part! We can, obviously, donate our time and compassion to those who need our presence. We can donate personal goods or even cars for tax deductions (one study from 2000 concluded that 733,000 people donated cars that year). At the least, these donations help clear out closets and recycle useful goods that are desperately needed by the poor. (Of course, one has to be wary of how much of the value of these goods actually reaches the charities. Always check to ensure your donation goes to a worthy organization who will distribute your generosity responsibly.)

As complicated beings, we possess many different needs and aspirations—human and religious—that seek to fulfill the need to give. Even when we are not driven by pure altruism, we are motivated, perhaps more significantly, by self-actualization, seeking a meaningful life, or religious fervor. Nevertheless, we can still do tremendous good for others. The perfect dare not be the enemy of the good. Reward is not to be the primary motive, but it is fine to accompany our giving. We are more concerned with helping others than perfect purity in motives. And, considering that, we are better people for it.

5.
WHEN ACTIVISTS HIJACK CAMPAIGNS, VITAL CAUSES SUFFER

Today, intersectionality in activism is clearer than ever, and systems of oppression are deeply interconnected. For this reason, it is tempting to connect reparations for black slavery in America to the treatment of animals in factory farms, or to affix the plight of Syrian refugees to that of undocumented immigrants from Latin America and beyond. But, animal rights activists, pro-life activists, or any other political campaigners should not use Holocaust or slavery imagery to talk about factory farming or their respective cause; Palestinians shouldn't hijack immigrant rights rallies and Israelis shouldn't turn "#BlackLivesMatter" into "#IsraeliLivesMatter" etc. While bringing attention to such issues is vital, it is wrong, however, for one movement to commandeer another constituency's narrative as their own, even where there may be fair comparisons.

This piggybacking disrespects other populations and their movements, thereby hurting the greater causes being advocated. Further, hisjacking campaigns breaks down trust in the social change landscape and alienates crucial allies.

My concern about this topic doesn't come from a vacuum. There have been several recent, escalating "hijackings" of political events. In August 2015, Senator Bernie Sanders, a Democratic candidate for the American Presidency in 2016, went to a large meeting in Seattle to defend Social Security against congressional Republicans who were trying to curtail the program. No sooner had he begun to speak than a woman identifying herself as a co-founder of Black Lives Matter Seattle seized the microphone, called for a prolonged period of silence for Michael Brown (whose killing by a Ferguson, Missouri police officer was a catalyst for the movement), and then began giving a speech. At that point, Senator Sanders left the stage and the entire rally came to an abrupt end.

Senator Sanders, who was an organizer for the Student Non-Violent Coordinating Committee (SNCC), had been arrested for protesting racial segregation, and had marched with the Rev. Dr. Martin Luther King, Jr., eventually came to an understanding with the group and other civil rights groups.

Conservative media, however, seized on this incident immediately. Indeed, FOX News still has a video on its website titled "'Black Lives Matter' activists hijack Bernie Sanders rally." RealClearPolitics, a right-leaning website, also prominently featured the event with the title: "'Black Lives Matter' Protesters Disrupt Bernie Sanders Event in Seattle, Sanders Gives Up the Mic to Them." While left-leaning media tended to favor Black Lives Matter, we may ask the question: Did this hijacking help the cause of Social Security, which in 2015 provided nearly $870 billion in benefits to more than 59 million Americans? Should we allow Social Security to be reduced, privatized, or even eliminated because some of its proponents do not agree with every just cause?

Conversely, libertarian anarchists (mostly aligned with reactionary militia movements), who oppose government ownership of land, experienced a hijacking of their own. In January 2016, a group of protesters in Burns, Oregon, protested the imprisonment of two men who were convicted of setting fires on land leased from the federal government. At its conclusion, a group of armed men hijacked the occasion by seizing unoccupied federal buildings at the nearby Malheur Federal Wildlife Refuge, led by sons of a Cliven Bundy, the Nevada rancher who had a long-running dispute with the federal government which resulted in a tense standoff in 2014. The Oregon protest organizers and the Burns Paiute tribe denounced the armed occupation, noting that the bird refuge established by President Theodore Roosevelt in 1908 was being harmed; no local support ensued. Harney County Sheriff David Ward emphatically stated that the armed occupiers were not helping the situation: It's time for you to leave our community, go home to your families and end this peacefully." Soon the original protest was forgotten, replaced by a media increasingly inclined to lampoon the incoherent rantings of the occupiers. Notably, one man who sat in a chair with a rifle on his lap, proclaiming that he thought there was a federal warrant for his arrest although he was not sure about that, donned a blue tarp that covered his entire body. Dubbed "Tarpman," he was ridiculed on social and international media. History will reflect whether this was a bad comedy or an act of domestic terrorism (albeit an ineffective one). Either way, no good ensued.

History shows many instances in which one cause was advanced to the disadvantage of another. Consider these examples:

- The Fourteenth Amendment, ratified in 1868, granted equality under the law specifically to men, and the Fifteenth Amendment granted the vote to black men. Susan B. Anthony and Elizabeth Cady Stanton argued that women should also be included, but other abolitionists and woman suffrage supporters such as Frederick Douglass and Julia Ward Howe thought that the compromise was necessary.

- President Franklin D. Roosevelt made a calculated decision to ignore racial civil rights during most of the New Deal. In exchange for this arrangements, southern Democrats helped pass critical New Deal legislation, such as Social Security, unemployment insurance, disability benefits, and the minimum wage.

While significant political injustice was tolerated in both cases, would we be better off today without these amendments or the essential New Deal legislation?

I think not.

I have attended countless protests clearly planned to address one issue when other groups emerge to insert their own chants. At numerous progressive rallies, Palestinian flags and chants emerge, for example. We all have causes dear to our hearts that may not be getting the attention we want. Does this give us the right to destroy other worthy causes? Should we interrupt a Black Lives Matter gathering to demand that the movement endorse the benefits of a vegan diet? Should we chant at abortion politics at a pro-education rally? We must remember the hard truth that the opposition to any worthy reform only has to get a majority of legislators to agree to oppose a single issue. If the proponents have a lengthy list of mandatory positions, the reforms will most often fail. While we would like to see sweeping change, there are times when we have to bow to pragmatism. We cannot deny intersectionality, but we must nonetheless show respect to each individual population combating their own unique oppression. Those of us involved with activism, should express our disapproval of those who hijack platforms not designed for them even when we agree with their cause. This will help bring integrity and equanimity back to our collaboration.

6.
THE MOST POWERFUL AND THE MOST VULNERABLE

Walking up the path to the White House is a humbling experience. Within those walls, history is made, affecting the lives of countless people. As the hub of American political power, the White House represents the best of what we want to achieve as a nation and the hope that springs eternal from the voices of the people. It is always a great honor to be a guest at the house on Pennsylvania Avenue. I have to remind myself that I have been privileged to be invited to the Hanukkah party that is held every year at the White House for all the years of President Barack Obama's administration. And this year, I was delighted to bring my friend Stan Hammerman, a model leader and the founding chairman of Valley Beit Midrash, as my guest to represent the Phoenix Jewish community.

Amidst the din of celebration and the gathering of the most significant Jewish figures in America today, the massive buffet tables of kosher food, and the constant flash of activity, there is also a quiet space to reflect. The story of Hanukkah and the ideals of the American experience are not so dissimilar: They both represent "liberty over tyranny, the rejection of persecution, and...the miracles that can happen even in our darkest hours," as it was so eloquently stated in the president's Hanukkah statement this year. While the practice of presidents recognizing Hanukkah at all is fairly recent in our history—the famous picture of Harry Truman with Prime Minster David Ben-Gurion and diplomat Abba Eban comes to mind—it was Jimmy Carter who, in 1979, began the presidential tradition of a public menorah (with the help of Chabad-Lubavitch of Washington, D.C.). Since then, the continuing presidential dedication—which started with President Bush in 2001 and continues with President Obama today—of spending a whole night celebrating the holiday is a sign that the Jewish experience in America continues to strengthen, becoming intertwined with the singular American ideal of tolerance and acceptance of all faiths and creeds.

Indeed, each year with the president at the White House Hanukkah party, my intuition is reaffirmed that our primary Jewish role in America must never be demanding what enhances the Jewish community.

Rather, our focus as Jews is contributing our best as members to American society to continue upholding the ideals we deem essential.

Sure, we must advocate for Israel and against anti-Semitism, but we have the special ability to use our collective influence to contribute beyond ourselves. As Hillel famously taught: "If I am not for myself, who will be for me? And if I am just for myself, what am I?" (*Ethics of the Fathers* 1:14). These words ring especially true at the epicenter of American identity, where great world leaders and humble citizens assemble together. It is a testament to the American democratic experiment that we are able to thrive in a nation that welcomes the poor, the immigrant, the refugee—that population that finds succor in the nation's ability to let people write their own destinies.

After the mingling is over, pleasantries exchanged, photos taken and the party is a wrap, I leave the White House reminding myself that true spiritual leadership occurs not inside the grand palace with the most powerful, but outside with the most meek and vulnerable. Hanukkah, at its most basic level, is about finding miracles in times of utter despair. In our own way, lighting the candles reminds us that we don't serve our Jewish community expecting reward or prestige.

No, we do it because we believe it is right. We don't build our community and follow our tradition out of fear or guilt. Rather, we do it because we wish to be better and contribute more.

We do it because we believe in the vitality of the Jewish people, as the ultimate outsiders throughout history yet being able today to enjoy one of our most joyous holidays both with the most powerful and with the most vulnerable. And that, indeed, is miraculous.

7.
THE STUDENT DEBT CRISIS: MAKE COLLEGE FREE

Are we making our kids our number one priority today or merely setting them up for failure?

The value of a college degree has long been acknowledged as the stepping stone to a stable future. There is a consensus that having a college degree is an asset, and, in today's economy, probably a necessity. While Senator Marco Rubio, a 2016 Presidential candidate, mused on the need for more welders at the expense of philosophers, the need for broad-minded citizens is crucial to the continuing robustness of American social capital. And yet, he may have a point, for there is a pernicious side of the Ivory Tower as well. It plagues millions of people whose only sin is attempting to broaden their horizons and improve their lives: its name is student loan debt.

While a university education affords the opportunity to develop critical thinking skills and acquaint oneself with knowledge, both practical and esoteric, there are also inherent, concomitant economic advantages. Federal government data shows that a rising level of education produces lower unemployment rates and corresponds to higher rates of personal income. Analyzing data from 2012, for example, we learn that college graduates earned 60 percent more than those with high school diplomas. The ever-rising cost of higher education, however, has put this option in jeopardy for many middle-class and lower income Americans. Current college costs now include high fees as well as tuition hikes every year. According to the College Board, the average tuition and fees for the 2015-16 academic year at public colleges varied from $9,410 (for in-state students) to $23,893 (for other students); private colleges average about $32,405. Compounding this, only a fraction of students earn a degree in the traditional four-year period. According to a study by Complete College America, fewer than 1 in 5 full-time students earn a Bachelor's degree in four years, and colleges now routinely expect students to take six years to earn their degree.

The resulting trends of the unfettered increase in student loan debt seem to be dire, as the sparse jobs available after graduation cannot keep up with these expenses. Consider these statistics:

- Today, 40 million Americans owe student loan debt, up from 29 million in 2008.

- The current amount of debt owed is now more than $1.2 trillion, quadruple the amount in 2004.

- The average current balance of debt is $29,000, but those graduating in 2014 had an average debt of more than $33,000.

- At the start of 2015, more than 60 percent of Americans with student debt were not making payments on time in a manner to reduce their debt. The majority are using strategies such as taking out further loans to pay off their current debt or deferring payment, and a further 17 percent have not kept up with loan payments.

- The three-year default rate in 2014 was 13.7 percent, with the average default around $14,000.

- Debt loads appear to increase with age. Those age 30-49 have an average debt of $31,000, and studies consistently show that the highest rates of nonpayment and default occur among those in their 30s.

- Currently, 2.1 million people age 60 owe student loans, which has tripled since 2004 and is 850 percent higher over the past decade. Their debt has more than quintupled and now totals $43 billion. Many are literally having loan payments deducted from their Social Security checks.

The after effects of the Great Recession continue to exacerbate the situation as well. In a federal government study, those making up to $40,000 annually who began paying back student debt in 2009 have only paid off a measly 3 percent of their debt. In addition, 60 percent either fell behind or defaulted on their debt, with the highest rate of default among those whose debt was $1,000-$5,000. One reason is that while the job market has recovered (mostly), the level of wages remains stagnant. Those who graduated college in 2014 and landed a job had widely divergent median incomes. Those majoring in the liberal arts earned slightly more than $36,000, while the overall average was nearly $45,500. Paying back a huge amount of debt is difficult, even this level; many are not this lucky. According to a report by the Economic Policy Institute, the unemployment rate among recent college graduates is 7.2 percent, but the rate of those who are employed but making low wages ("underemployment rate") is 14.9 percent. In addition, those "idled" (neither employed nor enrolled in education) among young college graduates is 10.5 percent. The report noted that college graduates have faced jobs with stagnant wages for years: "Due to young college graduates' limited job opportunities, stagnating wages, and the rising cost of higher education, college is becoming an increasingly difficult investment." This is undoubtedly a sad state of affairs, especially for a nation as prosperous and open to opportunity-making as ours.

Indeed, the resultant accumulation of debt has had a deleterious effect on the economy. A recent business survey of those age 18-35 found that 56 percent were putting off major purchases—a house, a car, even marriage—so that they could store long-term savings because of the need to pay off student loans. A further problem is that many are choosing careers solely due to monetary considerations, to the detriment of teaching, social work, and other beneficial careers. A National Bureau of Economic Research working paper noted: "We find that debt causes graduates to choose substantially higher-salary jobs and reduces the probability that students choose relatively low-paying 'public interest' jobs."

This is why I was so intrigued by 2016 Democratic presidential candidate Senator Bernie Sander's proposal for free tuition for public institutions of higher education. The notion certainly seemed far-fetched at first, but upon reflection it's a positive step in the right direction. Leaving people nearly penniless to pay of a college degree is nonsensical. To leave the rampant proliferation of debt to the next generation of college students is unconscionable and a real abdication of our moral obligations. And to his credit, Senator Sanders' hasn't left this plank as some campaign platitude, but has laid out an explanation on how to pay for his proposal: "The cost of this plan is fully paid for by imposing a tax of a fraction of a percent on Wall Street speculators who nearly destroyed the economy seven years ago."

The decision to impose a tax on the same industry that spurred the recent economic downturn is sound and one that, even though Senator Sanders was not elected President, would be one that future leaders should seek to emulate.

The education of future generations is an imperative of society, part of the social contract that is the foundation of country. It is a right, not an entitlement, but we have strayed from our ideals. We've been too easily swayed by loose money, high expectations and harsh realities. To right this path, we have to consider all options to bring down the cost of the university education. Opening up public colleges to more people by making tuition gratis (or close it) can be the spark need to bring a new energy into the engine of American greatness. On both moral and strategic levels, our kids must be our number one priority.

8.
ANGELS, MEN, AND GOVERNMENT:
BRINGING CIVILITY BACK TO THE POLITICAL DISCOURSE

Like many others caught up in the spectacle (some would say "carnival") that is the 2016 Presidential primary race, I found the posturing, jockeying, and humor (intentional or otherwise) following our election process this cycle most intriguing. And yet, for all the free entertainment and constant influx of breaking news in the horse race to be Commander-in-Chief, I wonder if the country's fascination with personality over substance has led to an unprecedented level of uncouth vitriol. While the toxic nature of politics is inherent to the system, have we hit a new kind of civil low owing to an addict's level of constant flow of fresh headlines, social media feed nourishment, and the quest for higher ratings? Are we alienating countless individuals who appreciate nuance from civic engagement who we need for a healthy democracy?

To be sure, it is vitally important who we, as a democratic society elect. Questions—from the electorate and, indeed, the media—about the track records, policy positions, and personal dispositions of those who seek the public office are of the utmost importance for an informed populace. During the past year, the American public has been bombarded with a seemingly endless list of infractions that are meant to display the inadequacies of those running for office: from Hillary Clinton's private email server, to Donald Trump's brusque remarks about Mexican immigrants, to Dr. Ben Carson's Proustian gaps in his personal history to Senator Bernie Sanders' unequivocal advocacy for his democratic socialist ideals. Each of these characteristics inherent to the candidates works for and against them, redoubts in a constant sea of oppositional attacks and hostile media bias. Because of this constant barrage, those with the fortitude to put themselves out there to lead should be commended.

Concurrently, I feel there are some candidates running for president this time around (who I shall not name) that I just cannot take seriously. And there are others who are beyond the pale: they represent the worse, most base aspects of our nation. At some point, however, we must ask ourselves: Is our obsession with this contest and our dismissal, perhaps even hatred (or at least an extremely potent distaste), of particular candidates making our political process worse? The problem is not just the politicians and their rhetoric but the toxic political culture that so many of us bolster and foster.

Now, of course, someone running to be a top official must expect the increased scrutiny, but to what limit? Our democratic system is important for its procedure and its ability to maintain a functioning state supported by the people through peaceful transfers of power. But there is also the societal aspect that is vital to our republic, namely in the development of a collective character that furthers the aspirations of every citizen. We seek not only to develop our state but also our society. Though we are still a year away from the 2016 election, I feel as if the American political experiment this time around has drifted towards incivility at the expense of cultivating the brightest amongst our ranks.

In *Ethics of the Fathers*, there is the following admonition: "Be careful with authorities, for they do not befriend a person except for their own sake. They appear as friends when they benefit from it, but they do not stand by a person in his time of need" (2:3). In the long arc of Jewish history, this verse was a blunt reminder to be wary of those who would seek the mantle of leadership for their own gain. Certainly, looking at this passage with respect to contemporary politics, one could construe this verse about politicians cynically (as many in the electorate already do). But this is counterproductive. We, as voters—as citizens—have to break the cycle of cynicism and work for the type of political system we deserve; we have all the necessary tools, so let's put them to use.

For those seeking a more positive discourse in our politics, this is what I see as steps towards positive change. We can all re-commit to sticking to the facts, not pernicious rumors; only using language that we feel would be fair to both our preferred and opposing candidate; and imagining that a candidate we strongly dislike as one of our relatives who we disagree with passionately but whom we still have much respect.

In the thirteenth century, Rabbi Yonah of Gerondi wrote: "If you see someone who has achieved a prominent position but whose behavior is inappropriate, do not say 'If I were in his place, I would not do as he does." You do not know what tomorrow will bring, and you are no different from him or anyone else. Perhaps that prestigious position would sway you as it has swayed him. Only when you reach his place and his position and overcome your own tendencies will you have the right to question his conduct.

Politicians are not immune from emotional shaming. As the pressure builds, the constant rebuke from all sides may harden them in ways that make them less compassionate and more ideologically narrow. This is the opposite of what, in my view, we need in our leaders.

As equally important are the people that elect those into office: we are not immune to the impact upon ourselves and our culture when we engage in diatribes and screeds in lieu of reasoned debate. Each of us in the political ecosystem is profoundly and importantly imperfect.

As James Madison wrote all those years ago, "If men were angels, no government would be necessary" (*Federalist* No. 51). We are flawed; the system is flawed. But that doesn't mean we should expect perfection of intellect and temperament from our politicians. As society is rapidly changing, for better or worse, and we hold the power to shape the future of this nation. The quest to make this a "more perfect union" is never-ending. For the sake of our children and grandchildren, let's cease our petulant attitude towards those running for the highest office in the land and begin pursuing a rational course of action that will have consequence for decades to come.

9.
CAN RELIGIOUS INSTITUTIONS BECOME SWEEPING FORCES FOR SOCIAL PROGRESS?

Religious institutions have, at times, been at the forefront of progress by engaging in forceful spiritual leadership. The engagement of Cesar Chavez and the United Farm Workers grape boycott in the 1960s, for example, was part phenomenal leadership, part righteous struggle. But where are we more than half a century later?

We have many past examples that continue to inspire us. While most Americans know the pivotal impact of Rev. Dr. Martin Luther King and the Southern Christian Leadership Conference in the Civil Rights Movement, there were many other figures who had prominent roles in similar religiously-inspired movements. Rev. Dr. Anna Howard Shaw (1847-1919), for example, overcame enormous discrimination and not only earned a medical degree from Boston University, but also was ordained a minister. Additionally, she was a formidable speaker, and lectured throughout the United States and Europe in favor of women's suffrage, temperance, and Progressive causes that she believed would relieve the exploitation of women. Typical of her inspirational oratory is this 1888 speech to the International Council of Women:

...let me in the name of my master say to the young women here today if you have a bit of truth, hold fast to that which God had given you; let no power, no injustice, no obstacle, no scorn, no opposition, let nothing extinguish the flame.

Subsequently, Rev. Dr. Shaw served as president of the largest women's suffrage group, the National American Woman Suffrage Association, from 1904-1915, when the cause was rapidly growing through successful endeavors. She summed up the strength that her faith had given her throughout her life: "Nothing bigger can come to a human being than to love a great Cause more than life itself, and to have the privilege throughout life of working for that Cause."

Unfortunately, even in America, radical actions against the poor and the vulnerable compel people of faith to act. In the last several years, North Carolina Governor Pat McCrory and his state's legislature, for example, have acted in concert to take extreme and reactionary measures against such people, refusing to expand Medicaid (preventing 500,000 from affordable health care), cutting the education budget by $1 billion, repealing the Earned Income Tax Credit (thereby raising taxes for 900,000 poor people) while cutting taxes on millionaires, cutting back unemployment benefits, and passing perhaps the most restrictive voter suppression law in the country.

In protest, thousands of North Carolinians began gathering at the state legislature in April 2013, with many committing acts civil disobedience to protest such actions taken by their government. This gathering morphed into a weekly event that has since been called the "Moral Monday" movement. The Rev. William Barber, President of the North Carolina NAACP and a leader of the Forward Together movement, helped inaugurate the weekly "Moral Monday" gatherings at the North Carolina state legislature, issuing a statement, "Why We Are Here Today" to lay out the rationale of the movement. Rev. Barber began with a religious theme:

The book of Micah asks us, "What does the Lord require of you? But to do justice, love mercy and walk humbly with God." It is in a spirit of openness to the prophet's question that we gather here as people of faith and citizens of North Carolina.

In seeking to restore voting rights, reduce mistreatment of the poor, and promote education, Rev. Barber concluded:

As people of faith, we understand that we have been called to be the voice of the voiceless and the shepherd of God's beloved community. What we do here today is only what any responsible shepherd does to alert God's flock to the presence of the predators of democracy.

Fortunately, though we may not be facing issues this dramatic in our local communities, we can still explore ways in which our faith inspires our public leadership. It is an imperative of all those who call themselves people of a principled faith to examine how far they are willing to go to protect those who are in the most desperate need. How can we ensure that every church, mosque, and synagogue pays its workers a living wage? Only uses contractors who belong to unions? Limits its animal product intake for the sake of human health, the environment, and animal welfare? Engages in eco-friendly activities? Is inclusive to its own minorities and disenfranchised members? Could religious institutions throughout America follow the North Carolina grassroots movement and institute a national "Moral Monday" movement?

In short, how do we ensure that religious institutions are robust engines for change and social progress like they once were? To be sure, I have witnessed many positive models today that are bold and transformative. I have been to churches near the Mexican/American border that offer asylum to poor immigrants. I've been involved with the creation and destruction of the Tav HaYosher, an ethical seal model that is given to kosher restaurants that demonstrate a commitment to not only following the laws of *kashrut*, but also worker fairness and justice. I've been in countless churches and synagogues that feed and house the homeless. Religious institutions are at the center of the #Black-LivesMatter movement.

Perhaps the greatest contribution religious leaders and spiritual institutions have to contribute in the twenty-first century is giving a practical and spiritual framework for people to understand moral living by ideal and example. For religion to, once again, be front and center on creating positive agitation for change, it must preach less and model more.

10.
THE WORLD IS STILL FLOODING

The world is still flooding. Massive inequality of status and wealth, climate endangerment, and bloody conflicts place the souls of all of God's creatures at risk. Will we follow Noah's example to work to reverse the trends of abuse and neglect and strive to show mercy and compassion to every creature? Jews are called upon to be a compassionate nation. Indeed, the rabbis consider mercy and compassion to be essential characteristics to being Jewish (*Beitzah* 32b). By fulfilling the Torah mandate of choosing love over hate, goodness over callousness, we can reinvest in our core humanity.

Noah, his family, and each of the animal species that were under the protection of the Ark were saved. Will we be chosen to survive the next flood that emerges?

It seems Noah could not have imagined a world without each animal existing in it. The *midrash* teaches that Noah not only heroically saved two from every species by bringing them onto the Ark, but also that on the ark itself, he was tirelessly running from one to the next to give them proper treatment and care. Reading the story of the flood each year should remind us that when we endeavor for a more redeemed world, we must prioritize care towards the most vulnerable beings on our planet. We have to foster a society that rewards sustainable and responsible producer and consumer activities while penalizing wanton destruction of the precious resources our planet provides.

Jewish prayer services are modeled to remind us of nature and our connection to it. As is says in the Talmud:

From where do we derive that we pray three times a day? R[abbi] Shemuel b. Nahmani said it corresponds to the three times that nature changes over creation.

In the morning, a person should say, "I thank You, O Lord, my God and God of my fathers, for having delivered me from darkness to light."

In the afternoon service, a person should say, "I thank You, O Lord, my God and God of my fathers, for just as I merited to see the sun in the east, so too have I merited to see the sun in the west."

In the evening, a person should say, "May it be Your will, O Lord, my God and God of my fathers, that just as in the past You have delivered me from darkness to light, so may You deliver I me now from darkness to light" (Jerusalem Talmud, *Berakhot* 4).

Each time of prayer serves as a reminder of how interwoven our existence is with our environment. A change in our external state calls for a change of our internal state.

Rabbi Joseph B. Soloveitchik famously distinguished between fate (*goral*) and destiny (*ye'ud*). Fate, the Rav taught, referred to the aspects of life that human beings are not able to control. Destiny, on the other hand, "[I]s an active existence in which one confronts the environment into which he is cast with an understanding of this uniqueness and value, freedom and capacity." According to the Rav, "One's mission in this world is to turn fate into destiny, an existence that is passive and influenced to an existence that is active and influential" (*Kol Dodi Dofek: Listen*, 5-6).

Furthermore, Reb Simcha Bunim of Peshischa famously taught that one should carry a note in each pocket. One would read "I am but dust and ashes" while the other read, "The world was created for me" (Genesis 18:27; *Sanhedrin* 4:5). We should remember that we are humble guests of this universe, not it's owners. But that doesn't mean we should shun our duties to act as agents of powerful change, with the ability to take serious action to consequential effect.

It is all too easy to get caught up in conformist consumer behaviors. But as the Daoist sage Lao Tzu taught: "Care about what other people think and you will always be their prisoner." We have to take the initiative to break free—spiritually—of public judgment. To be cutting-edge in this regard means transcending conventional consumer norms and looking beyond the immediate pleasure response. We have a shared fate, as Jews, as humans. But we dare not reside too long in the past. We must have the strength to take responsibility for our destiny together. We have to quell the flood. Each of us is called upon to exercise our unique leadership.

Like Noah, this is our sacred responsibility.

11.
A Plea For The Citizens of Syria

"Please. *Please.*"

Through tears and desperation, these were the words of a Syrian boy stopped by Hungarian border guards as his family tried to escape the horrors of the Syrian conflict and reach the safety of Europe. The manifold atrocities unleashed by the evils of the Assad government, and to a lesser extent Islamic State (ISIS) militants, have now caused catastrophic anguish and torment to millions of innocent people the likes of which we have not seen in generations. The ensuing Syrian refugee crisis has grown ever more present on the evening news, but this is only a symptom of something far more pernicious and heinous. Human beings have been turned into cannon fodder. This is a trauma that will not heal —externally or internally—for decades to come. The suffering of the Syrians is more traumatic than ever. It was incredibly disheartening for me to learn that in August 2015, nearly four years after the war began, Syria witnessed its bloodiest month of the entire conflict.

I'm still struggling to come to terms with the enormity of the situation, the seemingly utter hopelessness that blocks international action, prevents an end to violence, and delays the relief of countless souls. But I will not allow myself to become jaded. I cannot utter a prayer with integrity if I close my heart today to the cries of Syrian children, children like that Syrian refugee child in Hungary. In the years since Syrians began a revolution against their malevolent government, over 250,000 innocent people have lost their lives in chemical attacks and indiscriminate barrel bombings that destroyed houses, hospitals and schools alike. Targeting civilians—civilians created in God's image—has now become the norm rather than the exception for the Assad regime and ISIS. In this case, there is no more room for armchair philosophizing; there can be no more deferral to agreement by committee before working toward a meaningful resolution. We must "circumcise our hearts," awake to the cry of the Shofar, and act.

Therefore, to stave off additional bloodshed in the most atrocious human rights crisis of the world today, I and other likeminded groups are joining together for a call to action that our political leaders should heed: Now is the time to act! Any more dithering is akin to a death warrant for countless innocents.

The solution is clear, and we—the Jews for Human Rights in Syria, in solidarity with the Syrian American Council and the Coalition for a Democratic Syria—are calling for the United States and its international partners to immediately establish a coalition for a No-Fly Zone in Syrian airspace. A No-Fly Zone will protect civilians merely trying to survive the inhumanity of constant regime barrel bombs, which are the main killers of Syrian civilians. Stopping the killing must be a priority. Although our groups come from different faith traditions, our goal is just and clear: all life is worth protecting, no matter the cost.

To be clear, many of my colleagues and I are philosophically dovish and generally opposed to military engagement; too often have we seen its shortcomings. But the situation in Syria is sufficiently dire that military action is not only preferable, but morally justified. This is especially true now that Russia is co-leading these atrocities. Our conscience cries out for a better solution than war, but realistically, this is the only hope for peace.

And while the Syrian refugee crisis is certainly grave, I am reminded in times of the holy words found in Psalms: Rescue the poor and needy! Deliver them out of the hand of the wicked!

It is not enough to lobby for resettlement of 10,000 or even 100,000 Syrian refugees, although this will of course save lives. No, this is not enough, because it leaves 10 million Syrian refugees and internally displaced persons behind. Rather than emptying out the country, our hope is to stop the problem at its source: we must end the ceaseless bombing on population centers that has caused the refugee crisis. We must fulfill the dictum in Psalms to deliver the poor from the hands of the wicked.

When there is evil in our midst and when human lives are being destroyed for naught, our anger should be righteous and unrelenting. As citizens of a free country, it is our duty to speak for the voiceless, give succor to the suffering, and comfort those deprived of holy love. Let us rectify the evils of madmen with a clear policy to protect the vulnerable, and contact our elected representatives so that they know our feelings.

Let us do our part to bring light to this most incredible darkness, as my community just prayed with fervor on Yom Kippur: "And iniquity will keep silent, and every bit of evil will disappear like smoke, for You will remove tyrannical rule from the earth."

12.
PARSHAT SHOFTIM:
JUST COURTS OR MORE THAN JUST COURTS?

Throughout our history, the Jewish people have been dedicated to the study and implementation of rules of law. Our greatest sages debated the grandest and most particular realms of legal matters and many volumes of Jewish scholarship are dedicated to the intersection of law both secular and spiritual. Indeed, what we find in our holy texts is the underlying basis of a system that gives earthly humans the rules needed to adhere to the spiritual blueprints from heaven.

Parshat Shoftim opens with the commandment for the Israelites to establish courts and select officials in cities under their domain. Ibn Ezra explained that this precedes the previous *parsha* which ended with the commandment to come to Jerusalem three times a year to teach that it is not enough to have a central place that people occasionally visit. Rather justice is meant to be pervasive and embedded throughout every society that has the foresight to ground themselves in fairness and political equanimity (Deuteronomy 16:18). As it is, the rabbis taught that Israel was given three crowns: the crown of *priesthood*, the crown of *kingship*, and the crown of *Torah* (*Mechilta d'Rashbi* 19:6). There is to be a separation of powers and responsibilities between religious, governing, and judicial bodies, with different experts varying their roles in society, to complement one another and, sometimes, to acts as checks one another. The commandment for Jews to establish fair courts is also one of the Noahide laws for gentiles. The *Sefer haChinuch* taught that each of the seven laws of Noah laws may contain many sub-divisions of laws as well (*Mitzvah* 416). Rab-bi Moshe Feinstein, for example, argued that gentiles have a religious obligation to pray in times of distress (*Iggrot Moshe*, OC 2:25). Further, Ramban taught that the seventh law—the one that establishes just courts—actually branches into hundreds of laws to ensure justice in society. But these hundreds of sub-laws can actually be extended towards the infinite as justice means more than simply establishing courts to handle conflicts. It is not limited to a judicial branch to respond to wrongs nor is it limited to the legislative branch to create new laws. It is a *mitzvah* for the inter-personal realm, for each of us to not follow laws and merely obey the courts but also to pursue justice in our lives. As the most famous phrase in the *parsha* states: *tzedek tzedek tirdof*—Justice, Justice Shall You Pursue—an axiom that has been a clarion call for people throughout time. How do we individually respond to inequities? There is a role for government, courts, business, and religious institutions. But there is also a role for every individual to sacrifice some privilege for the dignity of the other, the stranger even.

In *New York Times* columnist David Brooks' book *The Road to Character*, he distinguishes between "résumé virtues" and "eulogy virtues." He points out that our society today emphasizes "résumé virtues" of meritocracy such as accomplishment, achievement, external success, and status. "Eulogy virtues," on the other hand, emphasize virtues such as humility, character, learning, and inner work. Both sets of virtues are important for *ish-tzedek* (a person who does acts of righteousness). One must be really concerned about public external results: alleviating poverty, bringing joy to the downtrodden, giving sight to the invisible people of society. But one must also become a *tzadkan* (a person who is inherently righteous) by taking up less space to create more for others, by giving credit to others, by enacting justice in the very private sphere. It becomes a part of one's being. This is an old philosophical tension been ethical consequentialism and virtue ethics.

Feeling that the world is just on some meta-level is not merely a moral issue but also a religious one. We know from basic psychology that we project our experiences from the earthly world into the heavenly world. If we experience the world as having a foundation of justice, we may be more likely to believe in a *just* God who has order in the world. If we are surrounded by pain, suffering, a land without a judge and with no order that we only interpret as fundamentally unjust in this world and the next world then it is may be more difficult to embrace an Omnipotent Being.

This is the reason why that, when we enact justice by publicly demonstrating that no individual should be left behind, we are not merely helping that individual in need. We are not only fulfilling the Torah mandate to enact justice, but we are also building confidence in a Divinely ordered world. Through the process of emulating Divine compassion, we seal it to its proper order.

13.
THE RELIGIOUS IMPERATIVE TO OPPOSE SOLITARY CONFINEMENT

In the Torah, there is only one type of individual who is banished completely from the community: he who has committed a wicked deed and is stricken with *tzaraat*, a Hebrew term that is often times understood as some enigmatic form of spiritual leprosy. I've been pondering lately about the meaning of this idiosyncratic biblical paradigm for punishment. To me, it seems that however painful the blemishes may be, the true pain of this condition is the separation from a functional community, to be shut off from routine human contact; to live in isolation forevermore is a stunted existence.

Conversely, though this particular spiritual remedy for a spiritual ailment is of an esoteric nature, its design seems more merciful than the contemporary ecosystem that favors punitive justice over rehabilitation. For even one with *tzaraat* could abide just beyond the settlement limits, a place where there could be introspection and this was for a limited time. The modern mantra of "Prisoners deserve what they get" is at odds with our society's need for compassion and respect for all human beings.

There is no doubt that, in the modern conception of the practice, solitary confinement is an abusive means of control over other human beings. Isolated from contact, those who are placed in solitary have their mental identities slowly eroded to the point of destruction. With their basic humanity stripped, the argument goes, these people are now safely removed from regular society and no longer a danger to the outside world. But internally, prisoners are now a hazard to themselves and later to others. More than a decade ago, clinicians working on the issue created a term for this condition: Special Housing Unit (SHU) syndrome. Those with SHU were considered to have the following symptoms:

- A predilection towards paranoia and insomnia
- Distorted perception of time
- Heightened feelings of inner rage and fear
- Increased suicidal tendencies

Indeed, those who survived the ordeal of open-ended time in solitary confinement leave their situation with prolonged feelings of lethargy and apathy, unable to build new relationships with others. Any hope to be rehabilitated into normative society evaporates during their forced hermitic punishment.

With certainty, Jewish values are strongly opposed to the ill-treatment of prisoners, no matter their crime. This extends to the barbaric practice of unchecked solitary confinement. While I would not be so naïve to suggest that individuals who pose a threat to society should not be confined, the ostentatious injustice that is so apparent with years-long stints in solitary goes beyond rehabilitative corrections and towards societal sadism. This is not the justice under law promised to us by our social contracts. This is not keeping society safe. This is power structures run amok. And it has to end.

Thankfully, there is progress on the horizon. In 2015 and 2016, President Barack Obama issued executive orders that moderately curbed some extreme examples of solitary confinement in federal prisons. The President's executive orders on the matter have primarily been focused on giving juveniles relief from solitary, giving many a second chance. In an editorial published by the *Washington Post*, President Obama wrote:

The United States is a nation of second chances, but the experience of solitary confinement too often undercuts that second chance. Those who do make it out often have trouble holding down jobs, reuniting with family and becoming productive members of society. Imagine having served your time and then being unable to hand change over to a customer or look your wife in the eye or hug your children.

This step, a modest one to be sure, is vital to the moral wellbeing of our nation. While it is easy to project a stance of toughness, it is challenging to stand up and say that all people need to be treated with a modicum of dignity. From a moral perspective—from a spiritual perceptive—it is the right thing to do.

While we can embrace solitude as a spiritual practice, forced isolation is not an acceptable model of criminal justice—from a Jewish perspective or otherwise. As we debate the merits of President Obama's executive order, it is imperative that religious communities continue to be at the vanguard for the struggle for human rights for every person. People cannot live in isolation even if they have broken the law. Justice and mercy are two sides of a scale, but we must become proficient in balancing them in a positive way. From the Jewish perspective, we can be motivated by the first existential statement about the human condition made in the Torah, when God uttered *lo tov heyot ha'adam levado*—one should not live alone. A passage from the Talmud reiterates this point, comparing a life filled with isolation and a lack of meaningful discourse to that of the eternal void: "Either friendship or death."

Being compassionate towards those who appear to not deserve compassion is a moral conundrum. And to be sure, advocating for their basic emotional needs can be a thankless task. Nevertheless, the legacy of holy writ, passed down through the millennia has imbued us with a spiritual prerogative to vouchsafe the inherent dignity of all human beings, even those who have transgressed the laws of society. For if we mistreat them, then we are no better as spiritual beings for it. We might even be ethical cowards or hypocrites, dilettantes in a field that needs dedicated spiritual activists. Solitary confinement, as an entity, is injurious to society. By immediately abolishing this cruel and ineffective practice, we can increase both mercy and justice in our prisons and in society.

14.
How To Combat Hate In Society

Like many who live in Phoenix, I'm a transplant. Although I was not born in the Grand Canyon State, among the cacti, Frank Lloyd Wright architecture, and dry heat, I have quickly been able to call Phoenix my home. It's wonderful to see all the potential that Arizona, and Phoenix in particular, has to offer: the revitalization of historic corridors, growth in opportunity for young people, and arts and cultural events that highlight the heterogeneity of our bustling metropolis. Most important, especially for people raising a young family like myself, there is hope that the city's best days are yet to come.

For all the beauty and diversity I see, however, there is a pernicious side that sometimes emerges in our city. Since I was appointed by Mayor Greg Stanton as a city commissioner on the Phoenix Human Relations Commission in 2015, I've seen it manifest in many forms: anti-immigrant sentiment, xenophobia against refugees, a certain recalcitrance to engage in meaningful dialogue across ethnic and racial groups.

In early 2016, I came across an announcement that there will be a white supremacist skinhead music festival in Tonopah later in that year, and it gave me pause. Any First Amendment arguments for the allowance of such a gathering, notwithstanding, how could such an abhorrent gathering take place? And considering all the beauty that this state displays to the world, how could something so ugly exist? Looking more broadly at our nation, how can we ensure that harmony between people is ensured, protected, and valued.

At times, it is not easy to reconcile living in a place where there are individuals who promote hate and bigotry over love and understanding. So it is all over the American landscape in the past several years, there have been numerous instances of unvarnished prejudice in Phoenix that have, sadly, made national headlines: bikers who protested during prayers at the Islamic Center, a pastor encouraging violence against the LGBT community, and a certain callousness toward the plight of innocent refugees attempting to flee violence and find peace in the bountiful land of America.

These examples, while certainly not indicative of the greater population of Phoenix, nor of Arizona, are still troublesome obstacles in the quest for a community enlightened by the virtues of tolerance and acceptance.

Is this the sort of society we want to leave to our children?

In the Talmud, one of the central texts in Judaism, there is a passage that underscores the determination for those who seek out other views in order to comprehend the knowledge inherent to all cultures: "Who is wise? The one who learns from every person" (*Ethics of the Fathers* 4:1).

I see in these words the precepts of an opening toward a grander vision for American society. In our struggle against hate, let us espouse an ethos of pluralism; where there is a gap in empathy, let us find the resolve to overcome societal myopia; when the forces of baseless animosity are hurled toward our brothers and sisters, let us make our voices known that we will not stand idly to watch their dignity violated. Whether it's Muslims, Jews, African Americans, Latino Americans, Asian Americans, Native Americans, recent immigrants, refugees of all stripes, veterans, the homeless or members of the LGBTQ community, we are all bound by our common humanity to rise above the petulant hatreds that are intended to divide us.

We are a society that is becoming increasingly committed to the dignity of all populations, sensitive to their needs and their aspirations. We need to be a beacon for others to emulate. We want to shake off the fettered image of this state as backwards. We want to rise from the cultural ashes to be a relevant and respected metropolis.

Let's start today.

Kidney Donation

1.
GIVE A KIDNEY, GET A CHECK

When I donated a kidney in the summer of 2015 to a total stranger, I wasn't thinking about market forces. I had simply realized that I couldn't bear to have two healthy kidneys while knowing that someone out there would certainly die of renal failure. When I was wheeled out of the hospital, I began wondering what could be done, economically or socially, to make more people open to the idea of organ donation.

It's illegal to buy and sell organs in the United States and the inflexibility of the market can be unbearable for someone hooked up to a dialysis machine. The problem isn't low supply—in the U.S., there are millions of kidneys that could be donated without any risks beyond those of any typical surgery—so much as overwhelming, unfilled demand. Kidney disease is common, but treating it with dialysis is effective for usually a decade at most, not to mention very costly. While there were more than 17,000 kidney transplants performed in the U.S. last year, about eight thousand people became too sick to receive one or died waiting for a transplant. Another 100,000 people ticked off another year on a waiting list, on which the average stay is about six years.

The simplest solution—paying healthy people for their organs—quickly becomes complicated. Opening organ donations to the free market, even with robust regulations, invites some concerns. Would desperately poor people be forced into selling their organs? Would unwilling people have their kidneys forcibly removed and then sold? These nightmare scenarios are probably overblown, but the idea of selling organs is knotted up with the idea of sovereignty over one's body.

Still, it's a cause that many people advocate for. Alvin Roth, a Nobel-winning economist, has seriously considered what a kidney market would look like. "I've become interested in the fact that it's against the law to pay for a kidney anywhere in the world," he told NPR. "But it's not against the law to remove financial disincentives." Roth has noted that steps could be taken so that hospitals could easily reimburse donors' costs, and then in turn be reimbursed through Medicare or private insurance. He says that, in the big picture, this would pay for itself, given how many people it would exempt from the costs of frequent dialysis and hospitalizations. Unfortunately, though, it won't be enough to assure donors they'll be reimbursed—they need a stronger incentive.

As distasteful as it seems to commodify organs, the current situation is simply too catastrophic not to change something. Defenders of the status quo should put aside their belief finding "the mixing of kidneys and cash repugnant" in order to help arrive at an alternative that will not leave millions dead.

Moreover, in the current unregulated system, the world's poor are being exploited *en masse*. As of 2010, one in every five kidneys transplanted each year originated in the black market. The vast majority of people currently selling their organs are poor and live in developing nations—many do so in order pay off their debts. When one of these people sells his or her kidney, the World Health Organization estimates, it will go for about $5,000. The brokers who buy them can then turn around and sell them for as much as $150,000. Though it may seem cold and dystopian to use a market to incentivize poor people to sell their body parts, the truth is that some of them are doing it anyway.

So, as unsavory as compensation for live-organ donations may seem, a highly-regulated global market with an emphasis on equitable compensation could allay these concerns, as well as ensuring that operations are performed safely. It would be important to make sure such a market doesn't devolve into "transplant tourism." But, if orchestrated properly, it could simultaneously satisfy the needs of wealthy countries with long waiting lists and poorer countries with rampant poverty.

Such a market is not just some nebulous item on the world's wish list—a successful regulated market currently exists in Iran, the only country in the world that allows paid donations. (Even though the words "donors" and "donations" may seem out of place in the context of transactions, these terms are commonly used when discussing compensation for organs.) In the 1990s, after years of war and economic slumps, the country decided to pay donors for kidneys rather than incur the healthcare expenses of treating people with kidney disease. Within a few years, the program eliminated the national waiting list for kidney transplants and these days, the black market is virtually nonexistent.

It works like this: Donors-to-be go to a regional office run by volunteers, receive medical testing, and then get matched with a potential recipient based on their blood type. If further tests go well, the donation proceeds. The government assumes any costs if recipients cannot pay for the kidney, and most surgeries take place in hospitals with university affiliation. As an added incentive, male donors are granted exemptions from military-service requirements.

The system is not without its limits. Iran bans paid transplants for most foreigners, and a lack of state funding has inhibited the program—due to high inflation, government payouts have decreased dramatically in value. Sometimes, poorer rural areas run out of funds and donors lack follow-up care.

Even with these flaws, kidney donation is much safer in Iran than in nearby countries, according to Farshad Fatemi, an economist at the Sharif University of Technology, in Tehran. If compensating donors were illegal, he told the *New York Times*, "We might be more like India or China and have illegal clinics ... where nobody looks after patients and donors."

The ban that most of the world has on paying donors—and the icky feeling that prevents many people from supporting such a system—doesn't entirely hold up to logic. As Mohammad Akbarpour, a research fellow at the University of Chicago, has observed, "[A]ccepting money to donate a kidney and save a life is repugnant, but accepting money for being a policeman or miner or soldier—all of which are statistically riskier than donating a kidney—is O.K." All told, Iran has implemented a system that eliminates the terror of waiting lists and the danger of the black markets. Another nation, one with more public funds, would probably be able to implement an even more effective program.

In America., people may finally be warming up to the idea. A recent survey of Americans by researchers from Argentina, Canada, and the U.S. published in the American Economic Review found that while barely half of respondents initially favored a system that would pay organ donors, the number rose significantly—to 71 percent—once those surveyed were given information about how the system would actually work. Perhaps if such a program were presented more clearly to the public, it'd be more widely supported. The country already has a strong donor culture—more than nine million Americans give blood annually—and with the proper system, we can intertwine our bodies, fairly and safely, in a way that might be able to save everyone involved.

2.
WE BADLY NEED MORE DONATED KIDNEYS. LET'S START PAYING FOR THEM

As you read in the previous chapter, I donated a kidney to a stranger who desperately needed one. I decided I could not morally justify living luxuriously with a back-up kidney when someone else would die without my help. I felt compelled, both by my religion and by my conscience, to sacrifice whatever I could to save another life. The procedure worked, and I am no worse for wear.

I was not financially compensated for my deed (nor would I have wanted to be). But the truth is that a well-regulated market where financial incentives could be offered could save the lives of countless people. Since kidney sales are illegal, they often occur underground, which drives the price up substantially per unit. The inherent unregulated and unsupervised nature of the market makes it difficult to pay such a price unless wealth or connections are in place. It causes terrible harm to the world's most vulnerable people. Bringing kidney sales out from the shadows could solve both of these problems by increasing the supply of kidneys at a reasonable price and safeguarding the easily exploitable poor.

The impoverished people who sell kidneys are rarely informed of the risks, and lack health insurance or adequate compensation. They are sometimes not paid at all because the transaction was initially illegal and seeking police recourse would be futile.

There is no doubt that the current unregulated, illegal network is abusive. Organ brokers make false promises—some tell donors that kidneys will grow back after being harvested—and subsequently earn enormous profits over their illegal transaction. The Nepalese village of Hokse, near Kathmandu, is a heart-rending example. It is known as the "Kidney Village", due to organ brokers persuading so many villagers to go to southern India, where each has sold a kidney to a foreigner to raise funds to pay debts or to support their families. Geeta, a young mother of four, sold one of her kidneys for the measly sum of $2,000; she used the funds to buy a small house for her family. Her pain was for nought: in April 2015, the earthquake that struck Nepal leveled her modest home.

Her family now lives in a structure made of corrugated iron and clear plastic wrap.

In this worst of all possible worlds, only black-market incentives are offered. Since underground organ sales are happening en masse, we must look deep inside and ask vital questions: how can we re-channel this exploitative industry to one that ensures the health of the donor? How can these people be adequately protected in the procedure in such a way that non-coercive consent is ensured? How can exorbitant profit opportunities for organ brokers be eliminated? How do we ensure a level playing field to ensure fair distribution of donated organs? Those who support the prohibition of offering incentives think it will prevent the enormous ills of this abusive black market. But like the prohibition of sex work, it has failed.

Miserably.

Though it would be nice if everyone would donate a kidney altruistically, we don't live in a utopia. And why should society require pure motives from one willing to take a health risk to save another's life? We don't expect altruism when paying firemen and policemen. We pay soldiers to fight wars, doctors to treat ill patients and researchers to work in labs handling the Ebola virus. So why should we be troubled by a penurious person being paid for a small medical risk that will save a life, especially considering the mortality rate for kidney donation is less than that of non-essential plastic surgery?

As a rabbi—as a human being who believes in the infinite dignity of the other—I believe saving human life is of utmost consequence. If most people will not donate altruistically, then incentivizing people by offering them compensation and benefits should be our ideal. It is vital that we correct today's exploitative status quo of underground donation trafficking. This will bring sanity to a system that needs it. We can save countless lives. This not a mere apothegm: it is something worth striving for.

Animal Welfare

1.
AN INTERFAITH COMPASSION MOVEMENT CAN CHANGE THE WORLD

There are so many reasons why an interfaith animal welfare movement with a more prominent voice has the potential to create powerful change.

Starting movements that create positive change for society is righteous, laborious work. In the cloistered worlds of plant-based diets and animal welfare advocacy, there is not enough collaboration for the greater good. People often look for their niche. This is perfectly understandable: Individuals have their chosen spheres of interest and comfort zones, and they want to dedicate their time to what they know best.

I am no exception. I have my own aspirations, of course, but as of late, the notion of building a broader universal vision for the animal welfare movement has struck me as the future of the cause. If we are going to truly make a difference in our efforts to reduce the cruelty and consumption foisted upon billions of innocent, sentient beings, then we're going to have to consolidate our efforts. Together, we could be a real force. As St. Francis of Assisi wrote centuries ago, "Not to hurt our humble brethren (i.e. the animals) is our first duty to them, but to stop there is not enough." For me, the most natural place to start this fortification of our movement is within our communities of faith.

To be sure, the vegan and animal rights communities are mostly secular movements. It is wonderful that so many secular individuals have taken up such an extraordinary cause, and religious vegans owe enormous gratitude to these pioneers. Religious vegans need to now take a bigger seat at the table and bring our views to the ongoing conversation and discussion. For as it says in the Bhagavad Gita: "One is dearest to God who has no enemies among the living beings, who is nonviolent to all creatures."

Fruitful Collaboration Between Faiths
Faith-based initiatives addressing animal welfare have been marginal due to the lack of fruitful collaboration between faiths. While each faith possesses unique and important qualities, it is in the area of bridge-building and demonstrating unity where we will be most powerful. Kant implores us to remember that: "He who is cruel to animals becomes hard also in

his dealings with men. We can judge the heart of a man by his treatment of animals." Religious communities must take this truth to heart and be among the first to step up and say "No!" to the perpetuation of cruelty towards other creatures. The rabbis taught that we must not only avoid the Biblical prohibition of causing pain to animals (*tzaar baalei chaim*) but that we should also seek to show compassion and even to learn from animals (*Eruvin* 100b).

Trusted Religious Leaders Have a Wide Reach
In our post-modern society, local communities and neighborhood bonds have weakened. Religious communities, on the other hand, are still strong and central in many places. When organized around a cause, religious communities have astronomical potential to impact not just individuals, but whole communities as well. Religious people are more likely to follow their authorities and communal norms. They are also more likely to show up at communal events on a consistent basis.

When the Pope talks about climate change, hundreds of millions of Catholics listen. When an authoritative and wise Rabbi talks about animal welfare, the Jewish community listens. When the President of the Mormon Church pronounces, his members listen. When an Imam spreads a declaration of peace, his congregation listens. When a Lama expounds a message of tranquility towards all, politicians listen. And so it will go until *all* have the chance to listen.

On a practical level, religious institutions and leaders have massive political influence, an influence that is needed to shift legislation from current cruel policies. The unfortunate legalization of so-called ag-gag laws—laws that curb the First Amendment rights of concerned citizens—were partly the result of too little political organization amongst animal welfare activists. Religious institutions and figures have the means and ability to influence legislators through old-fashioned methods like grassroots organizing, petitioning, and spreading awareness. Melding political sophistication with the sincere exercise of ideals could greatly advance the cause of passing animal welfare legislation around the nation. Indeed, around the world.

Animal welfare issues, framed in terms of the spiritual and the moral, are deeply powerful. They can awaken people to their ethical potential, and to a greater awareness of the injustices around them. Jeremy Bentham provided the pithiest query in this way: "The question is not Can they [animals] reason?, nor Can they talk?, but Can they suffer?" What is Bentham asking of us? Not to consider the financial value of animals, nor their utility towards humanity, but their inherent dignity to occupy the same safe and compassionate realm as humans. There is nothing more powerful than having people realize that we share a world with countless beautiful creatures, each with their own story and their own nobility. Countless people, through naiveté or passive willingness to ignore the broader implications of their actions, perpetuate a cruel, unjust system that treats creatures with a brutish sadism and a callousness that makes a stomach turn.

Calling on Friends and People of Faith to Band Together
Paul McCartney once said, "If slaughterhouses had glass walls, we would all be vegetarian." These beautiful words inspire me to call for a greater mission! I'm calling on friends and colleagues of faith to join together and tear down the walls of complacency and tribalism, and to bring clarity to the masses by combining old wisdom with new perspectives. We need to be more ambitious if we are to going to end the needless cruelty inflicted upon living creatures every minute.

We live in a singular time where the connection between faiths is closer than at any time in history. Let us seize the unique opportunity. Religious people also have a monumental role to play in fostering a more compassionate world that honors all life and protects all sentient beings. Let us not squander our resources. Let us unite under a banner of friendship, mutual respect, and the unyielding desire to ensure that Creation is respected and given the deference it truly deserves. To make this possible, it will require the humility of people of faith to create space for others and it will require the secular community to create space for those of faith. If we truly care more about building a more compassionate world than flexing our own identities, then we will come out of our corners into a broader arena to change the world together.

2.
Do Animals Have Legal Rights?

There is a quote attributed to Gandhi which states that "The greatness of a nation and its moral progress can be measured by the way its animals are treated." The way in which Western Civilization has neglected its duty to care for some of its most precious creatures reflects a callous attitude towards non-human life. This is especially true in legal settings. For example, in British common law, legal precedents established over many centuries by courts (rather than statutes) have primarily determined a variety of judicial rulings, including those that pertain to animals. One of the most widely-emulated positions around the world has been the ruling that animals have no rights. Cases of abuse against animals were considered an infringement upon the owner's right of property, meaning that the law does not recognize animals as having their own interests.

One of the earliest challenges to this precedent came from Jeremy Bentham, who, skeptical of the legal philosophy of Sir William Blackstone, the foremost exponent of the common law, established the philosophy now understood as Utilitarianism. As he observed the movement to abolish slavery during the French Revolution, Bentham began to question other abuses. In *An Introduction to the Principles of Morals and Legislation* (1789), he openly speculated on "when the rest of the animal creation may acquire those rights which never could have been withholden from them but by the hand of tyranny... The question is not, Can they reason? Can they talk? But, Can they suffer?" [see previous chapter].

In the United States, a major development occurred in the post-Civil War period. Henry Bergh, after witnessing the mistreatment of horses in Russia and encountering the Royal Society for the Prevention of Cruelty to Animals in England, founded the American Society for the Prevention of Cruelty to Animals (ASPCA) in New York in 1866. To Bergh, it was simply a "moral question" that the "mute servants of mankind" such as horses needed protection. The New York State legislature then gave the ASPCA the authority to investigate cases of animal cruelty and make arrests. Bergh helped close down many places where dog fighting (dog versus dog and also dog versus rats) had occurred, and even established an ambulance to evacuate disabled horses.

By the time of Bergh's death in 1888, nearly all states had passed laws against animal cruelty.

Throughout most of the twentieth century, changes in jurisprudential thought regarding animal abuse have been minuscule. Early state legislation merely limited human abuse of animals and excluded many institutions from penalties. Even the Federal Laboratory Animal Welfare Act of 1970 was primarily motivated by a desire to protect dog and cat owners from having their animals stolen and brought to laboratories. Only in 1976 was the law changed to protect laboratory animals from egregious mistreatment, although the experiments themselves were excluded from the law's protections.

The predominant attitude during this time was that animal experiments helped people live longer, and had helped in the development of penicillin and insulin and treatments for asthma, kidney disease, meningitis, and tuberculosis. Science seemed to know what it was doing, and courts were reluctant to interfere. There were a few critics during this period. Mark Twain (who once quipped: "The more I know about people, the better I like my dog") regarded any experiments on animals as unacceptably immoral, and wrote several articles denouncing the mistreatment of animals. He was among a small minority.

In the 1970s, two new books challenged the status quo. Gerald Carson (1899-1989), a former advertising executive who later turned to writing social histories and later served on the Advisory Board of *American Heritage* magazine, wrote *Men, Beasts, and Gods* in 1972. The book challenged the legality and moral validity of animal experiments. In one experiment Carson noted that the Air Force used pregnant monkeys to conduct crash tests, and declared the results "preliminary," so it would be repeated indefinitely. As Carson sardonically noted: "How many pregnant women are expected to fly military aircraft has not yet been disclosed." Philosopher and Princeton Professor Peter Singer wrote *Animal Liberation* (1975), and questioned the validity of most animal experiments, dismissing them as "trivial and obvious," that millions of animals could be spared if these experiments were eliminated. Singer adopts Bentham's suffering paradigm of utilitarianism: enormous animal suffering in these experiments outweighs whatever minor benefits might emerge from research.

Resistance to addressing animal abuse was often found most strongly among those championing the animal entertainment industry (zoos, circuses, aquaria, etc.) and human benefit industries (slaughterhouses, dairy factory farms, labs).

It still took some time before court cases on behalf of animals made it through the system. In the 1976 case of *Jones v. Beame*, individuals and animal welfare organizations were initially successful when they sued New York City over the cruel and abusive conditions existing at two of the city's zoos. Unfortunately, this ruling was overturned a year later on appeal (the "zone of interests," similar to "standing" to sue, was deemed not to apply), delaying the time when people could sue on behalf of animals to protect their welfare.

Things began to change in 1981, when Alex Pacheco, a founder of People for the Ethical Treatment of Animals (PETA), began an undercover job at a federally funded laboratory, the Institute for Behavioral Research in Silver Spring, Maryland. He encountered monkeys locked into cages with huge accumulations of urine and feces. The experiments, far from having any medical rationale, often consisted of cutting the spinal nerve until a limb was disabled; then the monkeys were shocked until they made an attempt to use their disabled limb. The monkeys frequently were not fed and experienced great pain from restraints and the experiments. Pacheco secretly documented the abuses and PETA began a decade-long legal battle. In the end, the case created precedents for the first arrest and conviction over abusive animal experiments, rescue of animals from abusive experimental labs, strengthening of the Animal Welfare Act, and even a Supreme Court victory for animal welfare.

Today, organizations such as the Animal Legal Defense Fund (ALDF) continue to pursue court cases on behalf of animal rights. The ALDF currently has about 25 cases pending (several with PETA and other organizations), ranging from court suits to prevent the mistreatment and killing of animals by private citizens or companies, requests for documents to guarantee that animals are treated fairly in city and state facilities and exhibitions, suits against federal agencies (such as the Food and Drug Administration and Department of Agriculture) over their failure to protect and even plans to kill animals. In spite of progress, millions of animals are tortured and abused through entertainment, experiments, or individual abuse.

Progress at limiting torture and abuse to animals is moving slowly but there is increased attention on the matter. It is clearly not enough to merely legislate against abuse as this approach has not won in the American courts. Is it not absurd that a corporation can be treated as a legal entity ("corporate personhood") but another non-human entity that actually has sentience, animals, cannot? Even if animals do not become legal agents that have rights that can be defended in courts of law, we must, at the very least, reinforce the legal duty not to abuse any sentient entity. To be sure, humans without functioning *nociception* (pain receptors) still have full rights since humans have rights beyond possession of sentience. Although animals may not be moral agents, they may, of course, still be moral subjects deserving of moral and legal consideration for "animals are hardly strangers to our courts."

Even if animals are not granted legal rights, they most certainly must be granted legal considerations. Further, even if we agree that humans and animals are fundamentally different, this conclusion does not give license for instrumental use and zealous abuse with no accountability. An animal does not have the same legal rights as a human but legal duties and considerations must nonetheless be emphasized. This duty is not due to the animal capacity for reason, speech, or language. Rather it is due to their significant sentience. If one feels pain, one has a right to be defended against that pain and we collectively have a duty to prevent that needless pain.

This is the time that our legislation and court rulings must advance in one form or another to adequately ensure our laws are just toward all sentient beings.

3.
On the Extinction of Animals, Climate Change, & Shiluach Ha'Kan

Every year around autumn time, we leave the comforts of our homes to live in *sukkot* (huts) to humble ourselves and to reconnect with our existential core in nature. The looming international climate change crisis should be embedded in our consciousness as we dwell outdoors.

Unfortunately, the issue has become demagogued and politicized, to the point of absurdity (in 2015, a congressman from Arizona boycotted the unique opportunity to hear the Pope speak in front of a joint session because of exhortations about tempering climate change). Yet, it must be acknowledged that climate change is a fact and here to stay. Peer-reviewed scientific journals indicate that more than 97 percent of current climate scientists are unanimous in their position that climate change is caused by humans. The scientific organizations that have publicly endorsed this position include the American Meteorological Society, the National Academy of Sciences (United States), the Geological Society of America, the American Chemical Society, and nearly two hundred international scientific organizations, including the World Health Organization, the World Meteorological Association, and the World Forestry Congress; worldwide, the scientific consensus on this resolute.

One of the tragic impacts of surface temperature increase is the potential extinction of manifold animal species. A majority of scientists believe the earth is now experiencing the sixth mass extinction in Earth's history, with extinctions occurring at 1,000 to 10,000 times the normal expected rate. While previous extinctions were caused by asteroids or volcanic eruption, nearly all of this mass extinction is being caused by human activity, including climate change. Some species, such as polar bears threatened due to the melting of Arctic sea ice, have long been recognized as endangered. However, diminutive animals are also threatened. The American pika (an animal that resembles a small rabbit) may become extinct solely due to global warming, as it lives only high up on mountains with cool and moist climates. As Earth warms, it will become extinct. Here are some other examples of the looming possibility of extinction:

About a third of about 6,300 species of amphibians face extinction due to their sensitivity to climate change, a rate that is 25,000 to more than 45,000 times greater than what would normally be expected.

It is estimated that about half of all mammal species—along with humans, they include gorillas, monkeys, and lemurs—are at risk of extinction from loss of habitat and climate change.

A World Wildlife Fund report, as analyzed by the Zoological Society of London, of more than 5,800 fish populations in the world's oceans concluded that the number of fish in the world's oceans has declined by nearly 50 percent since 1970, due to overfishing but also to rising ocean water temperatures due to global warming. In North America, the American Fisheries Society estimates that seven hundred species of fish are in danger of extinction, representing nearly 40 percent of all fish.

Trees are not exempt from climate change and the increasing extremes in weather. During the recent and severe drought in California, about twelve million trees have died, largely from pests taking advantage of trees weakened from lack of water. Incredibly, even the massive, seemingly invulnerable Sequoia trees, some of which have lived for several millennia, are showing unprecedented stress, including shedding leaves much earlier than usual.

As Jews, it is a sacred duty to reverse these terrifying trends. Indeed, there is a unique *mitzvah* addressing this situation of human-caused animal extinction. The Torah teaches that one must shoo away a mother bird before approaching her young (*Shiluach ha'kan*). Rabbeinu Bachya (commentary on Deuteronomy 22:7), Ralbag (ibid.), and the Sefer HaChinuch (#545) explained that the reason for this *mitzvah* is to prevent actions or even the perception of actions that might lead to the extinction of a species. The mother bird is to be left alone so she can re-produce offspring. To destroy both the mother bird and her kin is to wipe out a section of creation and that is deemed too destructive. While Jewish law allowed for the killing of animals in prescribed situations, it also mandated the humility and the compassion to protect all creatures and honor all in living existence that we encounter.

Thus it is our moral obligation to protect the beautiful Earth that we have inherited. To pollute it is to destroy its sanctity, to plunder it without forethought is folly. During the holiday of Sukkot, we should channel our inspired encounter with nature to address this most crucial issue of our time.

4.
Do You Blush?
Our Inner Light as Spiritual Animals

Charles Darwin was once asked about how humans are linked to the animals and, with all of our knowledge about evolution, there was still anything unique about being a human. Darwin answered, "Man is the only animal that blushes." To which Mark Twain retorted: "Sure, man is the only animal with good reason to blush."

Meditating on the importance of the blush can be a spiritual exercise: What are the physiological and spiritual dimensions of this seemingly innocent gesture? The vitalness of blushing indicates that the human being experiences vulnerability in recognizing moral failings and spiritual deficiencies. We have been endowed with such enormous mental and faithful capacities that we can crucially feel embarrassed when we ought to ("the blush") and when we fall short of our lofty potential.

So we are almost like animals (determined beings with a set nature), but we also possess the unique capacity to transcend our baser natures.

While we may—and should—blush at our misgivings, it is crucial to develop self-respect perhaps even a healthy sense of self-love. David Brooks, writing in his book *The Road to Character*, explored this philosophical tension:

Around the eighteenth century, moral realism found a rival in moral romanticism. While moral realists placed emphasis on inner weakness, moral romantics like Jean-Jacques Rousseau placed emphasis on our inner goodness. The realists distrusted the self and trusted institutions and customs outside the self; the romantics trusted the self and distrusted the conventions of the outer world. The realists believed in cultivation, civilization, and artifice; the romanticists believed in nature, the individual, and sincerity (244).

In Jewish philosophy, there is a stipulation that we embrace both the self and the other, private and public life, both our inner weakness and our inner goodness. Within our ontological reality is our custodianship of a good inclination (*yetzer tov*) that we must cultivate and an evil inclination (*yetzer hara*) that we must either destroy or channel towards righteousness. Primarily, we build off of our own inner light and goodness, normatively, from which we have been Divinely endowed to go out and make our world more compassionate and holy.

Rav Kook's poem *Or HaNer* developed the notion of how unique and precious each of our spiritual capabilities can be:

Everyone must know and understand
that within burns a lamp or candle.
No one's candle is like another's,
and no one lacks his or her own candle.
Everyone must know and understand
that it is their task to work to reveal the light of
that candle in the public realm.
And to ignite it until it is a great flame
And to illuminate the whole world.

It is our duty to illuminate the world. Together. We do this not through an alien fire, but with our own irreparably unique soul stations. For it is through our infinite capacity for spiritual uprightness that we are gifted the ability of blushing: and thus the gift of repairing the world.

5.
A Spiritual Perspective on a Plant-Based Diet

How can we, people who have sacrificed for a worthy cause, deepen the spiritual roots of our movement to make our commitments more meaningful and more sustainable? Developing veganism as a spiritual practice will not only benefit us personally, but will also strengthen us to make a greater difference in the world.

Looking out on the vast American food production culture, it is not difficult to find problems almost immediately. From the metropolises on the coasts to the Hopper-esque rolling plains of the interior, loud and gaudy advertisements for the latest innovations in fast-food meat blaze across the land. Their ubiquity is disheartening; their unavoidability is maddening. But even more so, it's the sheer number of ads—physical, digital, and material—which engenders a profound disconnection that lodges in the minds of so many compatriots. For these ads, so seemingly innocent, present a real impediment to comprehending this fact: behind all of the joy they seek to portray lurks a deeper cruelty, hidden from public view but widely known to exist. For every person enjoying a tasty bite of a hamburger or a stack of chicken nuggets, there is the knowledge that sentient creatures—made of sinews similar to those that make up the human being—were destroyed to produce that ill-gotten bounty.

In these ads we celebrate the remorseless cycle of pain for profit.

With this unfortunate fact at the forefront of many of our minds today, the importance of replacing the unforgiving brutality of factory farming with plant-based eating is becoming increasingly clear. Through outreach and discourse, the trend towards plants as the main staple of the diet is only beginning to catch on in America. As the movement grows, impediments have begun to multiply as false studies, new doctrines, stubborn habits, and powerful lobbies become more robust.

Three Spiritual Virtues to Consider
I have identified three virtues as potential launching pads for further introspection. It is my hope that they will serve as guideposts for cultivating deeper intentionality in our dietary choices. At the end of the day, we will recruit others to our lifestyle and cause not through rhetoric but through morally sensitive and spiritually rich modeling.

Gratitude — First and foremost, we can cultivate gratitude—a deep appreciation of our own existence and that our lives are inextricably interconnected with each other's. The focus of our gratitude thus shifts away from the self and toward the other, and it leads us to take responsibility and care for other humans, for animals, and for our fragile earth. Through these deep commitments, we can further deepen our gratitude that we have the knowledge and resources to do what we know is right.

Discipline — Secondly, we can expand our capacity for discipline. It is not always easy to eat healthfully and ethically when the prevailing culture amplifies bad choices and willfully ignorant cruelty. The temptations surround us. They reach us through every medium of communication. Yet, there is also something simple (not easy, but simple) to the act of committing one's self to a lofty ideal. In doing so, we transcend our basest natures to become beings of compassion and potential. As we hone this sense of self, the discipline we accrue carries over into other important facets of our lives, from exercise to relationships to work and even to recreation.

Humility — Thirdly, and most importantly, we can develop a deep sense of humility. When we step back from the daily grind and focus on the grander meaning of the universe, we can arrive at the insight that the world was created not only for us and that we are not entitled to eat whatever we wish. Grasping this idea brings forth a beautiful, empowering conviction, one that embeds itself deeply into our consciousness. But we cannot let our newfound perspective blind us to kindness and respect for others. Acting and speaking self-righteously with those who have not (yet) arrived at the same resolve to adopt a plant-based diet is folly. I have come to learn, through the consequences of my own early zeal for the cause, that work performed in humility is far more likely to win the day. And such humility, when practiced with consistent authenticity, can be transformed to utter joy. Accepting that we will eventually pass from this world and nonetheless striving to make it more a compassionate and sustainable place is in and of itself a lofty goal worthy of aspiration.

At present our movement is rightfully concerned with the outer world: with animal welfare, with human health, with carbon footprints, and so forth. These are undoubtedly worthy values to embed in our awareness of the broader outer world. But, at the same time, I want to assert the equal importance of cultivating our resilient inner worlds. If we are to influence others, we have to improve and elevate ourselves. Deepening our spiritual and moral integrity by reflecting upon and eliminating any vestiges of inconsistency between what we believe and how we live is a wonderful practice for growing individually and building community. Together, we can enrich ourselves and one another.

Every year at Yom Kippur, I am reminded of a traditional explanation for why we do not wear leather shoes on a day where we reflect on our self-growth: how can we seek compassion from above when we, at that moment, are not acting compassionately, wearing the remains of a tortured and slaughtered creature upon our feet? In the liturgy of the day, we ask "Who shall live and who shall die (in the coming year)?". Indeed, that answer is in large part determined by the choices we ourselves make.

So, let's choose life together.

May we live long and live well.

Interfaith Partnerships

1.
A Gathering of Global Faith Leaders:
My Experience at the Parliament of World Religion

The crush of religious people I witnessed was staggering. Under one roof, a tapestry of faiths flock together—Buddhists, Christians, Sikhs, Muslims, Humanists, Jews—congregated in a singular location to discuss some of the most pressing matters facing humanity today. But for every external difference of faith I see, this conference is harmonious. People are in good spirits. In Salt Lake City, I attended my first Parliament of the World Religions—the largest inter-religious conference in the world—and I was moved by what I witnessed.

For those thinking that the Parliament is meant to decipher ancient papyrus scrolls or new hermeneutical approaches to arcane medieval spiritual literature, little could be further from the truth. Indeed, this wildly diverse spiritual jamboree focuses less on the minutia of theology and concentrates more on issues related to social progress. Themes like climate change, war, and income inequality were more the topics of discussion than dogma, exegesis, and apologetics.

Begun in Chicago in 1893, the Parliament was created as a means to foster global dialogue amongst faith traditions. The particular conference I attended was only the fifth gathering since its inception and the first in the United States in two decades. Impressively, the Parliament gathers some 10,000 participants from eighty countries representing fifty spiritual or faith traditions. But more impactful than the actual content of the learning sessions was the melodious and sensuous vibe of the gathering. Along the hallways I found people dancing. I found people in deep meditation. I heard heavenly music and smelled mystical scents.

The gathering halls and conference rooms all give emanation to the similar sense: ring of song, the solemnity of chant, and the echo of laughter. Unity of the spirit is in celebration in this holy space.

I was at the epicenter of a spiritual clarion call!

I was not sure what would happen going into the Parliament. But I have come out inspired! Experiencing the cross-section of human potential in one place opened my eyes to start seeing religious folk as more than points on a graph. Every different faith is like a sibling. And each type of sibling has their own characteristic that makes them distinct, from the goody-two-shoes to the one who wants to rebel against the world, the one whom everyone loves and the one who lashes out. But as the eminent biologist Jane Goodall remarked during the closing ceremony of the Parliament: "When we all get together and consolidate and cooperate, instead of fighting, we're gonna save the world."

Each faith has a different role to play. We may not always agree, indeed we may not even like each other, but as distant family we have to stick close together. From time to time, it's good to re-connect—a family reunion, let's say—even though we spend the majority of our time separate and with our immediate relatives.

As I left the conference and headed back to my hotel room, I walked away with feelings that I didn't know I would have when I walked in. The whole experience shifted my perception of inter-religious relationships. We shouldn't shun our differences, but use our contrasting philosophies to tackle the most pressing challenges facing the world. When we look deeper into the souls of compatriots, we come away with the knowledge that we have so much in common. We should celebrate it. It's nice to remember that though our faiths take us on different paths, they can all ultimately take us to the same destination.

Religion, when an engine for collaboration to address social problems, is a source for tremendous optimism about our collective destiny.

2.
Towards Jewish-Christian Reconciliation & Partnership

Jews are a history-oriented people. And the history of the Jewish people has been filled with baseless bigotry and deep-seated religious suspicion, culminating in devastating tragedy. Central to Jewish historical consciousness is Christian anti-Semitic persecution throughout the millennia. The legacy of Jewish humiliation and religious persecution is grim: medieval massacres of Jews by Crusaders, hostile disputations in the High Middle ages when Jews were compelled to defend their faith against attempted mass conversion by the Church to no avail. During the devastation wrought by bubonic plague, Jews were accused of poisoning the wells. In response, countless were massacred and displaced across Europe. Already reeling from baseless hatred, Spanish Jews were forced to endure the ignominy and brutality of the Inquisition. Ultimately, many were tortured, killed, banished—their dignity and assets confiscated.

By the nineteenth and early twentieth centuries, Russian pogroms (sanctioned attacks against Jews) grew in magnitude: In 1905 there were nearly seven hundred pogroms; more than three hundred Jews were murdered in Odessa alone. In 1919, Ukrainian army units massacred 2,300 Jews in two days, while White and Red Army units murdered thousands of Jews and burned down their towns.

The most significant catastrophe in modern history began with indifference and collaboration of many Christians: the Holocaust. Pope Pius XII's Concordat with the nascent Nazi regime had disastrous effects, legitimizing the Nazi regime and undercutting the last consequential resistance to Nazi rule in the Reichstag. Pius XII issued no public protest to Nazi atrocities during the war. In October 1943, more than a thousand Jews in Rome were rounded up for transport to Birkenau and again no protest was heard from the Vatican; the overwhelming majority of the two thousand Jews transported from Rome were murdered.

The Catholic Church's change in perspective towards the Jews only emerged post-Holocaust. In 1958, Pope John XXIII quickly moved to modify Catholic prayer to eliminate anti-Semitic references. In 1960, the pope told Jewish leaders: "We are all sons of the same heavenly Father. Among us there must ever be the brightness of love and its practice." Later that year, he put the topic of repairing relations with Jews on the agenda of the Second Vatican Council. In 1965 the Council adopted *Nostra Aetate* ("In Our Time"), which condemned anti-Semitism, urged a "dialogue of mutual esteem" with Jews, and repudiated hostile doctrines that the Church had replaced the Jewish people as well as claims of deicide, that Jews were responsible for the killing of Jesus.

Pope John Paul II did much to further reconciliation. He stated —repeatedly—that anti-Semitism is both a crime and a sin against God. Under his papacy, the Holy See recognized Israel, and in 2000 he visited Yad Vashem and the Western Wall, apologizing for Church persecution of Jews and praying for the welfare of the Jewish people, who remain the "people of God's covenant." John Paul's work has been taken up in earnest by the incumbent Pope Francis (who counts among his friends Rabbi Abraham Skorka of Argentina). He is the first Pope ordained after the promulgation of Nostra Aetate and, while archbishop of Buenos Aires, had a warm relationship with the Jewish community. In December 2015, the Vatican issued a statement that Catholics should combat anti-Semitism and that the Church has no institutional mission to convert Jews. In January 2016, Francis commemorated two events in Rome: the day when Roman Jews were deported by the Nazis in 1943, and the 1982 attack on the Great Synagogue of Rome when Palestinian terrorists perpetrated the largest anti-Semitic attack in Europe of the post-war period.

Now, history is going in a new direction. Thankfully, five decades after *Nostra Aetate*, the reconciliation between Jews and Christians continues to strengthen!

The rapprochement between faith traditions is the basis of a heartening 2015 statement just released on the website of the Center for Jewish-Christian Understanding & Cooperation (CJCUC) in Israel. What makes it all the more extraordinary is that the statement is signed by leading Orthodox rabbinic luminaries who break away from the apathy that haunts normative Orthodox attitudes on interfaith matters. The opening lines—"We seek to do the will of our Father in Heaven by accepting the hand offered to us by our Christian brothers and sisters. Jews and Christians must work together as partners to address the moral challenges of our era"—indicates that the statement is the most profoundly Jewish-centered interfaith documents ever to be released.

The Orthodox Rabbis' statement, which I proudly signed, doesn't patronize its readers with platitudes about coming together for its own sake. Instead, it acknowledges that the noble faith communities have had centuries of antagonism but that now is the time to overcome past enmity and cooperate under the Godly imperative to repair the world: "Both Jews and Christians have a common covenantal mission to perfect the world under the sovereignty of the Almighty, so that all humanity will call on His name and abominations will be removed from the earth."

I found most moving the passage from the heart of the document. In a mere economy of lines, the ruptures of history and a path for a bright future are laid to bare:

We Jews and Christians have more in common than what divides us: the ethical monotheism of Abraham; the relationship with the One Creator of Heaven and Earth, Who loves and cares for all of us; Jewish Sacred Scriptures; a belief in a binding tradition; and the values of life, family, compassionate righteousness, justice, inalienable freedom, universal love and ultimate world peace.

I was moved by my fellow rabbis' commitment to moving beyond what divides the faiths and move towards those aspects of commonality and mutual respect. This is a step forward in the right direction, for Jews and Christians alike. We have so much farther to go in our journey. And yet, the sustained endurance of this holy Abrahamic partnership begins today.

Within the Orthodox Community

1.
WHY WE SHOULD STOP BASHING THE ULTRA-ORTHODOX COMMUNITY

In recent years, a certain story in the daily news has become routine: A pious man won't sit next to a woman on the airplane; a learned holy man states that a flood is caused by homosexuality; a press release states that all religious approaches outside of their own are lies; a little girl is spit upon for not being dressed modestly enough to a man's standard.

Based on these episodes and many others, one might deduce that these were the results of a fanatical religious cult. But the truth is that these were the actions of Jews. Or more precisely, Haredi (ultra-Orthodox) Jews who hold the commandments of Jewish law to the most stringent reading.

Ever more prominently in the secular news and throughout Jewish conversations worldwide, there seems to be a broader movement amongst some in the Jewish world to position themselves in contrast to the "Ultra-Orthodox" Jewish community. Attention to this once-insular Jewish population is becoming more prevalent in media with portrayals making many people uncomfortable, myself included (especially since I was once immersed in the Ultra-Orthodox community and I continue to have deep ties and relationships in that world). Too often, the critiques I hear of this community are unfruitful, unrelenting bashing. There are a number of reasons this should stop. While many positions and actions from pockets of the Haredi community may drive us mad, perhaps our question is: How should we react to them?

Firstly, we should cultivate more gratitude toward the Ultra-Orthodox for what we gain and learn from them. Although their industries are far from perfect, the greater Jewish community often relies heavily upon this community for kosher certification, *mohalim*, reliable minyanim for those saying *kaddish*, maintenance of *mikvaot* and *eruvin*, publishing helpful books and placement of educators in schools, and the writing of sacred scrolls. Additionally, we have much to learn about their deep commitment to Torah observance, passion for Jewish learning, fervent prayer lives, and often unparalleled *middot*—character traits like modesty and humility— and the kindness they demonstrate within their community. The fact that we disagree ideologically on many points and object to many of their particular exclusivist practices should not get in the way of learning from these other facets. Further, our pluralistic ethos need not pause before those who claim certainty in holding the absolute exclusive truth and reject us as valid Jews seeking to block us from full participation in Jewish life. Even as they bash us for our modern commitments, we can ignore these rants and humbly take the high moral road.

Secondly, they pose no threat to us; we need not be intimidated by them. While the Haredi community may be growing in numbers due to higher birthrates, they are concurrently declining in influence. Pre-modern approaches will not be intellectually persuasive with moderns and certainly not with post-moderns. The more they reject new ideas—university study, autonomy, Zionism, feminism, diverse sexual orientations, inclusivity, social justice, meaningful relationships with gentiles—the less influence they will have on broader Jewish life (Israel excluded, where there are real financial burdens since the state supports the ultra-Orthodox lifestyle financially). Not offering a competing voice in societal discourse, their positions can be respectfully ignored.

Finally, bashing the "Ultra-Orthodox" position is simply erecting a straw man. It is easy to knock down fundamentalist positions without asking the hard questions about our own positions and without growing in our own convictions and practices. We have the obligation to avoid all distractions in our striving to serve God and in our developing our own authentic path to advancing Torah.

The truths and wisdom that are present in this community should be understood and evaluated fairly, rather than dismissed. For too many modern Jews, the only interactions they have with their Haredi compatriots is through negative media stories and smear campaigns. While it would be foolish to deny there have been some acts taken by this community that are reprehensible—*Agunot* (women chained in unwanted marriage) are told to wait for the Messiah to be redeemed, for example—it is certainly our imperative to not overlook the broader virtues that are to be found there.

Let me be clear: we continue to have the task of addressing moral violations where we have the potential to influence better outcomes. Yet merely bashing those with totally different sensitivities will not help them or us. We must learn the delicate balance between ensuring that Judaism is not singularly represented by their models, but also not falling into a trap of obsessive, knee-jerk, myopic outrage. Tolerance of beliefs and practices is ideal, but not at the detriment of letting bad behavior that misrepresents the Jewish people proceed unchecked. We would be failing Torah by not letting Ultra-Orthodoxy know when there have been deep breaches of social decorum but, by and large, our approach should always be sensitive respectful criticism.

It is my deep conviction that the Creator moves society toward progress and that Torah is the guiding light in the process. Our task is to discern what is morally right from what is morally easy. This said, we must be honest before God and have the humility to embrace that we are all fallible and that every faction has its virtues and vices. We should primarily turn our critique inward and not outward. Further, our approach should be to learn from the virtues of every group and softly and respectfully critique the vices only in the rare opportunities where we feel morally compelled and can make a difference. We should strive for friendship and partnership when opportunities arise.

2.
CAN ORTHODOXY GET BACK ON TRACK?

As a rabbi who has found my place to be within Modern Orthodoxy, I find religious life particularly powerful and meaningful. Balancing the modern and the timeless presents its challenges, but the beauty of Modern Orthodoxy is that it provided me with the critical life framework I needed to flourish and serve as I strive to navigate a complex world. Indeed, it is the only way I know how to live.

Yet, for the all the wonder and joy I experience in celebrating the observant Jewish way of life, I feel that we must be honest: Orthodoxy—like any denomination or ideological group—is laden with multitudinous challenges that must be addressed honestly, openly, and with a candor that allows us to grow as individuals and as a community. Leaders of every faith and denomination have a sacred responsibility not only to support their community but also to foster a culture of internal critique and avoid defensive arrogance.

I love Orthodoxy, but it is in crisis.

Some advocates of following the demanding rigors of Orthodox life tell others who perform outreach that Orthodoxy — as a construct — has the essentials of perfection, a contemporary panacea. In this view, there are certain strictures of Orthodoxy that are sacrosanct, specifically that this strain of Judaism holds the absolute truth, that everyone who enters the movement becomes happy, and that Orthodox religious life is a stress-free pathway to overall contentment. Indeed, many, including myself, find deep meaning, connection, and community in Orthodox life; yet sadly, the idealized form of a perfect Judaism does not match reality. This is a big part of why so many have physically remained but spiritually disengaged or simply left altogether.

While there are unparalleled acts of *chesed* (kindness) within Orthodoxy, the Orthodox in-fighting is similarly un-paralleled for its personal vituperation towards others in the community. I suspect that there is no Jewish denomination that regularly uses as much toxic rhetoric and aggressive vindictiveness as we see within Orthodoxy, especially on internet chat boards and comment sections. What causes all this meanness eludes me, but it is profoundly disturbing. The existential crisis of Orthodox Judaism today is not that we have cultural divisions and a plethora of problems that we disagree on how to resolve.

On the contrary, it's often productive to have different ideologies and serious disagreement. Our real problem is that our frequent hostility and arrogance are destroying us as a community.

This is obvious in a number of areas: the brewing crisis regarding women's leadership and the extent to which women are invited to demonstrate leadership in the community; the integrity of the *kashrut* system's ethical standards has been called into question; our broken conversion system that continues to leave countless converts (and people in the process of converting) with the shame of unnecessary exclusion; we have not yet cleaned up the heart-rending problem of *agunot*, those women chained in marriages against their will; and so many of our Orthodox day schools, which are in financial and pedagogical crises. We further need to grapple with serious problems of poverty, lack of secular education, cultural isolation, and health (an Ultra-Orthodox Jew in Israel, for example, is seven times more likely to be obese than a secular Israeli Jew). These are but a few of the challenges that Orthodoxy faces. They themselves are not the existential threat, but rather the toxic discourse surrounding them threatens implosion. There are vast numbers of people in the community who are either apathetic to these challenges or who are stubbornly opposed to any discussion of them. We betray the community when we don't courageously collaborate due to tangential ideological disagreements.

Many of our fears get channeled into petty wars driven by fear-based leadership, while a shortage of emotional intelligence and behavioral discipline prevent us from engaging in civil discourse and respectful disagreement. It is as if our house is all aflame and everyone is arguing about what color the carpet should be. Who among our Orthodox leaders today is soaring above the politics and addressing our profound problems in a respectful way that brings more light than heat? Who is modeling our cherished *mussar* tradition of working on oneself and collaboratively and humbly solving problems across divides before blaming another ideological camp for their faults?

To be sure this is not a new problem. Rav Kook, who served as teh first Ashkenazi Chief Rabbi of pre-state Israel, was so hated by some camps that some poured garbage on his head when he walked the streets of Jerusalem. Rav Joseph B. Soloveitchik, the spiritual leader of Modern Orthodoxy and Yeshiva University, was so disrespected by some Orthodox leaders that they refused to call him 'Rabbi'.

We cannot merely continue to tweak the marketing of Orthodoxy when our product itself is breaking. Our community is unable to avoid political differences that make it impossible to fulfill our larger collective goal of *avodat Hashem* (love of God) through *Torat Yisrael, Am Yisrael*, and *Eretz Yisrael*.

If the vast numbers of people refuse to discuss the basic causes that underlie these issues, then the vitality so essential to transmitting religious intellectual life from one generation to the next is at risk of becoming only a footnote of history. Like all of us, I desperately want to avoid this.

For me, Orthodox Judaism is the apex of merging ritual, philosophy, action, and love of my fellow human being. I cannot imagine leaving this community. Its commitment to a Divine Torah and Jewish law is unswerving, and its diligence for prayer and Torah study astounds me while the piety of humble Torah scholars inspires me.

For all that is right and meaningful with the community, we must be honest and admit that Orthodoxy is now facing an urgent existential crisis that affects us at our core. Those of us who care about the community need to muster the courage to meet these challenges openly, even if it means feeling the caustic sting of our colleagues and peers. If that is what needs to happen, then so be it. We should call for greater humility in the Orthodox community and commit ourselves to face its problems while checking our defensiveness, territorial instincts, and triumphant illusions at the door.

This would be a modest, but crucial, first step.

There is no shame in publicly admitting that we are struggling. Only by overcoming our communal fears can we engage with and display greater tolerance toward those who disagree with us.

3.
THE CHIEF RABBINATE:
TZIMTZUM AND HITPASHTUT

For millennia, the Jewish people were dispersed across the face of the earth, no single place to call their home. There were always dreams, of course, where Jews could one day congregate, free from violence and intimidation based solely on their practices and beliefs. And ever since 1948, when Israel was founded, there has been a locus for Jewish life to reside, where innovative religious thinking can be fostered, and where values so long suffused in the Jewish psyche could be brought to the fore.

While religious life in modern Israel always existed, until recently it was more often than not cordoned off from the more negative dealings with the state. Separation between religious authorities and those in the government, while never disconnected, often had more narrow spheres of influence. This is no longer the case. And sadly, while it hurts to admit it, there has been a corrupting influence that has seeped into what should be the sacrosanct elements of our religious leaders: unchecked spiritual power.

Most depressingly, the repercussions of this need for more consolidated power has affected the one authority that should be immune from such abhorrent concerns: the Chief Rabbinate.

I do not intend to suggest that the totality of the Chief Rabbinate is in some way malevolent or unable to handle their clerical duties. In fact, beyond a shadow of a doubt, the Chief Rabbinate means to do well; to do well by the Jewish people is akin to doing all in service to the Heavenly realms we wish to serve. They wish to be the gatekeepers of a unified Jewish people, they wish for a strong identity for the state of Israel and for all of global Jewry to look at Israel as the paragon of a functioning contemporary Jewish state. In essence, they seek to preserve the purity of the nation. They feel terrified of the change occurring in society and wish to slow it down and control it. Despite what are obviously good intentions, the Rabbinate—rightly or wrongly— has caused (and continues to cause) irreparable harm to the Jewish people, causing thousands of vulnerable souls to become alienated from Israel, even more, they have alienated countless people from Judaism and living a Jewish life. This problem is not merely relegated to ideology or politics. This is an issue of *middot*, or more precisely, not deploying *middot* (virtues) in a conducive, productive manner. From a *kabalistic* perspective, we are seeing others fall into the trap of misapplied *hitpashtut* (self-expansion without limitations) and the inability to be *metzamtzem* (retract to make room for others).

When Judaism, indeed religion, explores its most negative proclivities, it abandons the Divine model of *tzimtzum*: creating space for others to lead and to choose, even to err. Today, it seems we are merely witnesses to a group that seems on the verge of conquering as much space and power as possible to make room for their singular view of moral purity. This is one of the great challenges that strikes at the heart of Jewish life in post-modernity. It is one of the challenges that is causing major rifts within the fabric of our culture. I fear it is one of the challenges that our children and grandchildren will still have to overcome.

We need not run from this challenge. Rav Yakov Yosef of Polonne, the eighteenth century disciple of the Baal Shem Tov, wrote:

> Talmudic scholars and righteous people must not declare that they have no need for the masses just because they are the pillars of the Torah. Nor must the masses be arrogant, declaring that they have no need for the talmudic scholars because those scholars depend on the masses' financial support. At the individual and social levels, both the material and the spiritual are needed in order to create a whole person (*Commentary* on Exodus 30: 11-16).

Rather than abandon hope of an overbearing religious bureaucracy, we have been blessed by the ability to question everything. Why is this body acting without transparency and nuance? Why does the Rabbinate not feel that they are accountable to the people they are supposed to serve? Why are those fleeing Judaism being pushed away rather than being brought back in with hearts full of love? We have our obligations to vouchsafe the legacy of our ancestors, many of whom perished without reason or logic. Why now, when the Jewish people have more incentive than ever to love each other is there an official body that seeks to divide the souls of a great nation? It is here that we will struggle. It is here where we will seek justice. It is here that the children of Abraham will know that our voices will be heard. Rather than dwell on the challenges of religion and state in Israel, we can turn the question back to ourselves. Within our souls the answers lay, ready to be opened for our hearts to accept them.

By rejecting the Chief Rabbinate, as it operates, we are not rejecting the rabbinic establishment. Rather, we are in need of once again rebuilding trust and love between rabbinic establishments and the laity. To do so, each of us must check our own over-extended *hitpashtut* and ensure that we are not trying to control others or take up too much space in oppressive ways. Indeed, this is a spiritual journey each of must embark upon to build the future of our people.

4.
ORTHODOXY SHOULD EMBRACE INTERFAITH FAMILIES

I believe that religion—and Judaism—matters. And because I believe that it matters, I also believe that one should marry another person with shared values, whether it's ethics, theology, and even ideology (to a certain degree). Those values are inextricably linked to our personal and social narratives.

We are all aware of the challenges that the culture of intermarriage presents the Jewish people. Many in the Jewish world were dismayed by the 2013 Pew Research Center survey that indicated intermarriage had increased for most Jewish denominations in America. Among Jews who married since the turn of the millennium, a majority (58 percent) had married someone of a different faith or of no faith. This compares with the period before 1970, when only 17 percent of Jews who married had married partners from another faith or of no faith. While 56 percent of married Jews currently have a Jewish spouse, there is a vast difference between those who are religious (64 percent) and those who are not (21 percent). In addition (among the denominations surveyed), there was a correlation between the percent with a Jewish spouse and the level of traditional observance (98 percent of Orthodox Jews, 73 percent of Conservative Jews, 50 percent of Reform Jews, 31 percent of Jews with no stated denomination).

For many, the data was alarming, or at least a call to action, especially in contrast with Israel, where the intermarriage rate is about 5 percent. In their analysis of the Pew survey, Professors Jack Wertheimer and Steven M. Cohen of the Jewish Theological Seminary and Hebrew Union College-Jewish Institute of Religion, respectively, saw this trend as threatening Jewish identity in America:

...as many as [2.1 million] Americans of some Jewish parentage—overwhelmingly, the offspring of intermarried parents—do not identify themselves as Jews.... intermarried families are considerably less likely to join synagogues, contribute to Jewish charities, identify strongly with Israel, observe Jewish religious rituals, or befriend other Jews.... the large majority of intermarried families are loosely, ambivalently, or not at all connected to Jewish life.

Professors Wertheimer and Cohen stated further that this effect multiplies over generations. Only about 20 percent of intermarried parents raise their children solely within the sphere of the Jewish religion, and these children marry gentiles in slightly higher numbers (83 percent). In turn, 92 percent of their children will marry gentiles, so that only 8 percent of intermarried grandchildren will remain in the religion of their ancestors.

On the other hand, intermarriage is within our zeitgeist and exists among the broader population in America as well. A 2015 Pew Research Center survey indicated that 39 percent of Americans who married from 2010-2014 married outside their religion. Among gentiles between the years 2010-2014, 18 percent of Christians married spouses with no religious affiliation, 15 percent married Christians from a different denomination, and 6 percent married spouses with other religious affiliation, versus lower percentages of those who married from 1960-1969. Some groups have high rates of marrying (or living with a partner) of the same religion: Hindus (91 percent), Mormons (82 percent), and Muslims (79 percent). While Jews lag somewhat behind at 65 percent, this is a higher percentage than mainline Protestant groups (59 percent); one could easily understand how cultural and religious differences might preclude Hindu and Muslim intermarriage.

Rabbi Rick Jacobs—currently the President of the Union for Reform Judaism—compared opposition to intermarriage with opposition to gravity, as both are inevitable:

…I still hear Jewish leaders talk about intermarriage as if it were a disease. It is not. It is a result of the open society that no one here wants to close. The sociology is clear enough; anti-Semitism is down; Jews feel welcome; we mix easily with others; Jewish North Americans (researchers say) are more admired overall than any other religious group. So of course you get high intermarriage rates—the norm, incidentally, in the third or fourth generation of other ethnic groups as well.

For Rabbi Jacobs, there is a realistic duty to welcome gentiles who marry Jews:

We have a sacred obligation to open our doors, to add to our ranks, and to make sure that progressive Judaism has a growing, not a shrinking, voice in proclaiming what Torah must mean for our time and for our world. It is a veritable gift of God to have the opportunity of a millennium: more non-Jews who want "in" than Jews who want "out." That has never happened before. We dare not squander this gift out of fear of what new voices may say and where new opinions may lead.

While opponents keep their distance from those who intermarry for fear of encouraging more intermarriage, Rabbi Jacobs considers intermarriage an opportunity to expand the Jewish community, thereby involving more people in the process of Jewish education. These divergent opinions by learned scholars are not without their particular compelling arguments. How does one balance a desire to retain the richness of Jewish tradition without ostracizing so many from the community? While the Reform Movement goes way too far for Orthodox standards, the more traditional can still learn from the culture of embrace.

My commitment to pluralism outside of the home is rock solid. Inside the home though, internal strengthening supersedes foundational diversity. For this reason, I, like all Orthodox rabbis, would not encourage nor would I officiate a marriage between a Jew and a gentile. I also wouldn't support a marriage between a Christian and a Muslim or a believer and an atheist. How we interpret the moral and spiritual order of the world is too significant. Liberal Jews who choose not be affiliated with Judaism might rebut that they find their values elsewhere and share as much with liberal Christians as they do with liberal Jews. But where will they turn for life cycle milestones, holidays, and spiritual language? What traditions will they embrace in the home once they have children?

A full embrace of intermarriage or any type of moral and theological relativism won't work for those of us who believe faith, ritual, and community deeply matter. When someone dies and a child wants to know how they'll mourn, what will they be told? When exploring complicated questions about truth, how will they be advised? If one later returns to their faith in a fervent manner, will they need to get divorced? When a person of religious commitment replies, we can have questions and answers. Judaism supplies a unique spiritual and moral anchor to our people and our history.

Values matter. How one mourns matters. Spiritual language matters. Building families and raising children around grounded values, beliefs, and traditions matters.

Bearing this in mind, I believe the Jewish community still has a long way to go to support intermarried couples. While I would not conduct one of these marriage ceremonies, I embrace the idea that intermarried families—including the spouse of another faith—are a crucial part of the Jewish community and they deserve respect. For them, Judaism as a religion may not be of primary importance, but they are still a part of our people and culture.

I have heard too many stories from intermarried families of how they feel alienated and marginalized. Many spouses from other faiths feel that they're valued only if they convert. They may not be Jews, but they should be treated as members of the broader Jewish community. Naturally, there will always be some barriers for attendees who don't embrace the beliefs, language, or practices but we should strive for warmth wherever possible.

We are no longer in the Middle Ages where social exclusion policies are an effective (or more morally responsible) tool for those with different theological conclusions from us.

Christianity should not be viewed as the threat to American Jewish life it once was. The real threat today is materialism: those who choose nicer cars, more vacations, and longer work hours over spiritual and ethical commitments. We are not losing Jews to church but to real estate.

Like any marginalized population, it is not enough to treat them like everyone else. Rather, we have to go above and beyond to embrace and support interfaith families to compensate for their internalized sense of marginalization and for their actual experiences of alienation.

I have a special connection to this issue: I was raised in an interfaith family. This is to say that I would not exist if it were not for intermarriage. I'm grateful for my upbringing. I was exposed both to Christianity and Judaism in my early years in respectful and supportive ways (ceremoniously, educationally and spiritually). In the end, through destiny or fate, I embraced Judaism in the fullest sense. I felt richer for full exposure and for the opportunity to make deep and complicated decisions. I chose my journey in an open and tolerant environment. Had I been treated with hostility as the child of an interfaith family, I might not have embraced Judaism and certainly not have become a rabbi.

At the same time, I am saddened that few in similar circumstances will have the same fortunate experience as me. Most have shared that they simply don't value religion because the message they received from their parents was that religion didn't matter. You can be X or Y or Z; it's all good. Just be a nice person, it doesn't matter what you believe in or where you locate your moral consciousness from. It is, of course, true that atheists and those without religious affiliations can be moral individuals. Secular humanists and existentialists have contributed immensely to human progress, but I fervently believe that Judaism has unique contributions that are crucial to moral development.

We are stuck knowing that intermarriage most commonly hurts the Jewish community but also knowing that we must embrace these couples who have made this choice compassionately and openly. Intermarriage is going to happen regardless of our views, but we have to be ready to face the challenges and opportunities that come with it rationally and lovingly. Each human being has infinite dignity and should be embrace warmly and inclusively. Further, in the twenty-first century, every Jewish community should (and must) amiably embrace all couples that are searching for Judaism in their meaning-making journey.

5.
Religious Pedagogues Should Embrace Liberal Education

When I was studying in a yeshiva in Jerusalem, I'll never forget the poster that hung above my bed. It read: "Don't be so open minded that your brain falls out." They, like most conservatively-oriented religious institutions in the world, were attempting to promote an approach that suggested authority to their truth while conveying caution against critical, autonomous thinking. I've often thought about that quote and what it means in relation to the state of contemporary education.

For millennia, religious education mirrored general education. It subscribed to an authoritative transmission of information, where questions were not as welcomed as they should have been. In modernity, leaders in education embraced a more liberal approach to education (I mean this not in the partisan sense, of course, but in the philosophical sense), that encouraged autonomy, critical thinking, democratic values, and empowerment placed on the students. Students would not simply be told to accept "truths" to memorize, but would be partners in an open discovery of their subjects.

John Dewey (1859-1952) was a major force in twentieth century American education, and his reforms were contemporaneous with the nascent Progressive movement. To Dewey, education should mirror the best of a democratic society. Thusly, rote learning of an archaic, remote curriculum needed to be replaced with a system where students participated in a relevant curriculum to learn by doing (a philosophy called Pragmatism). In his book *The School and Society* (published 1899), Dewey viewed school as "an embryonic life" that was imbued with the classical liberal disciplines of "art, history and science."

According to Dewey, each child is brought into this "little community... with the spirit of service, and... with instruments of effective self-direction... we shall have the deepest and best guarantee of a larger society which is worthy, lovely and harmonious." In addition, this community was heterogeneous: "Only diversity makes change and progress" (*Democracy and Education*; 1917).

The American heartland, a bastion of traditionalism and suspicion, did not accept this cosmopolitan, tolerant educational system. Foreigners, and foreign ideas in general, were distrusted, and in 1921 and 1924 immigration quotas were made increasingly stringent, with the feeling that the newer immigrants did not embody American values. When the Ku Klux Klan was at full strength with millions of members, their brand of fundamentalist Protestant Christianity (which shunned and despised minority populations) constituted a powerful political bloc that few were brave enough to cross; this ideological view seeped into certain parts of the educational ecosystem. Indeed, education was affected by laws attempting to curtail new ideas, most prominent a Tennessee law that forbade the teaching of any doctrine about creation other than that found in a literal read of the Book of Genesis. In the ensuing Scopes trial (some would say circus) of 1925, prominent attorney Clarence Darrow squared off against former Democratic Presidential candidate William Jennings Bryan in a debate about the merits of evolution versus creationism in public school classrooms. While some viewed the trial as a triumph of science, it took another forty years for evolution to return as a staple in Tennessee classrooms.

Looking at today, Christian schools with a strict interpretation of Biblical precepts require that students and faculty adhere to an often narrow range of behaviors inside and outside of school. Look to the example of Larycia Hawkins, a tenured associate professor of political science at Wheaton College, an evangelical institution, who was placed on administrative leave and dismissed for writing on social media her belief that Christians and Muslims "worship the same God." The college, which fired another professor for converting to Catholicism, requires its faculty to affirm the college's statement of faith, which is interpreted conservatively. Professor Hawkins had previously been required to reaffirm the statement when a photo emerged of her at a Chicago home on the day of the Chicago Gay Pride parade. Professor Susan M. Shaw of Oregon State University, who had taught at two conservative Christian colleges, commented on the situation by noting that fundamentalist colleges have grown less tolerant in recent years, and questioned the consequences of suppressing theological discussion: "What is lost when theological dissent is not accepted or even welcomed?" She saw the school's policies as a sign of spiritual weakness:

Faith that is threatened by hard questions and differing opinions seems to me not to be faith at all but rather a rigid system of belief that can abide no challenge and makes no room for the God who is still speaking.

A starker contrast in the philosophy of religious education is evident in the Muslim world, with the disturbing emergence of fundamentalist Muslim factions controlling education. The predominantly Pashtun Taliban first emerged in northern Pakistan after the failed Soviet military campaign in Afghanistan. Many within the Taliban had gone to religious schools (madrassas) in Pakistan and while there, had learned the uncompromisingly strict Wahhabi Islamic theology from the Saudis who supported these schools. (In short, the Wahhabi view of Islam is the belief that the Quran must be interpreted literally, and that anyone who does not follow their beliefs—including other Muslims—are evil and must be fought and eliminated.) When the Taliban seized control of Afghanistan in the late 1990s, they conducted public executions, forced women to wear garments that covered their entire body (burqa), and arrested men whose beards were not long enough. In 2001, in spite of worldwide protest, the Taliban destroyed the huge Bamiyan Buddha statues in Afghanistan, which they deemed blasphemous.

While the Taliban was ascendant in Afghanistan, in 1997 Malala Yousafzai was born in northwest Pakistan. Her father, Ziauddin, ran a school and was an advocate for universal education in a nation among the highest in unschooled children. From an early age, Malala shared her father's passion for education. When she was 12, Malala began writing a secret blog in favor of education for girls. The Taliban, who controlled large swaths of Pakistan and forbade education for girls (or for women to go out by themselves), told Ziauddin to close his school, and when Malala garnered worldwide attention for her campaign for girls' education, they targeted her life. In October 2012, a Taliban assassin boarded the van that she and her classmates took to school, and called her out by name before shooting Malala, whose skull was fractured by the bullet. Revulsion over the cowardly attack led Pakistan to pass the Right to Free and Compulsory Education Bill. For her efforts and sacrifice, Malala became the youngest recipient of the Nobel Peace Prize. She has used the award money to help fund schools for girls, including one near the Lebanon-Syria border that will provide education to over 200 girls who would not otherwise have access to education. As Malala said in a 2013 interview: "[T]he best way to fight against terrorism and extremism is just [a] simple thing: educate the next generation."

While Malala opposed the Taliban, she is a proud Muslim, and is named after a Pashtun heroine, Malalai of Maiwand, and has also cited (and used as her pseudonym) the legendary Gul Makai, a Pashtun who use the Quran to convince the men around her to renounce war.

She said: "The Taliban think we are not Muslims, but we are. We believe in God more than they do, and we trust him to protect us." In addition, in the manner of the best students, she does not always share the opinions of those who support her. In an October 2013 meeting with President Obama, Malala told him that: "Drone attacks are fueling terrorism" by killing innocent people and thus building up resentment against the United States.

While not as dire, the traditional education experienced by most ultra-Orthodox (Haredi) Jews has its own negative consequences. A 2015 Pew Research Center update on Jews in America disclosed the following: Among the ultra-Orthodox, 38 percent achieved a high school education or less, compared with 15 percent of other Jews. 43 percent of ultra-Orthodox Jews had an annual household income less than $50,000, compared with 31 percent of other Jews. In addition, 45 percent of ultra-Orthodox Jews said that all of their friends were Jews (compared with 13 percent of Modern Orthodox and 2 percent of other Jews). Ultra-Orthodox Jews also have more children and have distinctly more closed social perspectives than other Jews.

Consequently, traditional religious education that avoids contact with the outside world, and limits exposure to a modicum of secular subjects, has distinct disadvantages in the ever complicated infrastructure of contemporary life. Although this goes beyond economic impact, we cannot dismiss the burden placed upon families and society for raising large families without proper secular education, job training, or nuanced perspectives on societal matters.

But it is not only the most extreme among our religions that are still embracing a traditional approach to education rather than a liberal approach. Traditional religious education is still pervasive throughout religious America. This is not only impairing cognitive and spiritual development but it is also deeply alienating to students who are surrounded by a broader culture that embraces open, inclusive, democratic educational discourse. We cannot afford to lose more people from religion because our authoritarian learning models are too rigid. It is understandable that we'll have some fear of encouraging students to discuss and think for themselves without shoving the truth down their throats and we will indeed lose some students, but in the end, the gain of empowering and honoring students is far greater for them, for our communities, and for the future of the ideas that we cherish.

Today, many religious institutions have still not embraced the notion of liberal education. There is an ongoing fear that allowing students to think for themeslves will lead them towards the "wrong options. This is a mistake. Religious institutions have to see the dignity in students and honor their right to make choices and to think critically and openly. Disagreements should be part of the process, but they must be understood in context. Discouraging honest debate is the antithesis to an informed student body. And should the students be misinformed, how will they grow up to be productive citizens?

When religious pedagogy becomes more open and inclusive, the benefit will be great: fully-rounded people willing to change the world for the better. And our religious institutions will only flourish with a more open, inclusive, and intellectually nuanced approach. This is a challenge that every religious institution must consider.

Personal Growth & Relationships

1.
SPIRITUAL AWAKENINGS: LEARNING TO TRUST OURSELVES

When we open our souls in prayer, we open our hearts to a Divine relationship. Not only that, we open our minds to a type of decision-making, where we take ownership and responsibility for our own lives. While seemingly an effortless task, the process of prayer requires a lot of work: it takes listening, fine-tuning, meditating, learning, and re-creating the conscious self. This is certainly not easy, but the results pay dividends. With only one life to live, we must reclaim this deliberate existence: our own existence in service of a lofty heavenly mission and a pragmatic earthly task.

The Kotzker Rebbe asked: "If the heavenly gates of tears are never closed, why are there gates at all?" I'd humbly like to propose an answer to this thoughtful question. I'd suggest they're a mere projection of the gates around our own hearts. Who among us has not experienced pain and been numbed and hardened by the world? In removing barriers from our hearts, we can meaningfully support others. A person who is suffering is like a burning temple waiting to have the fire put out; to be rebuilt with love. It is an imperative to rebuild our inner palaces, those that have become fenced off. We can do it each day! It only takes perspicacity and grit to strive for this lofty goal to be achieved.

We also must learn the proper balance in our lives between pragmatic life and spiritual life. Ever feel like at every moment you're urgently called above toward spirituality and below toward pressing human pursuits? Yehuda Amichai—the Israel Prize winning poet—articulated this challenge well:

Taxis below
And angels above
Are impatient.
At one and the same time
They call me
With a terrible voice.
I'm coming, I am
Coming,
I'm coming down,
I'm coming up!

There is no perfect objective balance; it is relative to each of our lives; we must learn to trust ourselves. The great *mussar* teacher, Rabbi Yerucham Levovitz, asked "Who is the best Torah commentator?" Rashi? Ramban? No! Rav Yerucham suggested it's You! Torah only works if we construct personal meaning, own it and internalize it. So too, spiritual navigation works only when we cultivate the inner world, when we take the time to tend to our souls, and we learn to trust our inner Godliness.

We still need spiritual teachers and guides, but ultimately we must be-come our own teachers and guides as well living by faith, conscience, and inspiration. No one can inspire us if our hearts and souls aren't open to inspiration.

It is important, thus, to embrace the notion that our spiritual decisions may not "make sense." Prayer doesn't mock our sense of reason, it transcends our reason! It is this access to a deeper truth that makes it possible for us to live a spiritual life in a temporal world.

2.
STRENGTHENING OUR FAMILIES: ARE YOU PREPARED TO REJECT SEDUCTION?

"I made a mistake." "It was all so fast."

Sadly, in my career as a rabbi, I have seen far too many families shattered because of shortsighted pursuits of pleasure. Often good people, why are they acting in such a destructive manner?

It only takes one moment.

Only one moment before an entire life's foundation can be shattered and moral potential cut short. The lures of forbidden romance, so often the stuff of lurid paperbacks and soap opera pabulum, are not often discussed openly in a manner that speaks to the moral character of our friends, family, and colleagues. Yet, it is important to consider the consequences of an affair, the ramifications it has on society, the harm it causes familial structure, the pain it causes one's partner, and the irreparable damage it causes to one's life journey.

We are overdue for a collective conversation about one of the greatest social ills of our time; one we are all aware of but less are adequately prepared to handle. Families are tragically broken every day from infidelity. The moment one decides they will accept or reject seduction is a momentous one. A tempting opportunity is presented with a co-worker, friend, or prostitute, and a lifetime spent learning ethical decisions is at stake.

A moment of self-indulged pleasure can result in a lifetime of lingering disasters. Sometimes— heroically—families get put back together. More often than not however, family units are destroyed. Most will, in theory, say they are opposed to committing adultery. But what is needed is that every man and woman in a committed relationship be prepared for how they will reject a seducer. Ethical commitment isn't enough. If one knows they struggle with temptations in general, they should meet with a counselor to prepare themselves. Further, one must remove fantasies from one's mind to ensure that in a moment of test, one doesn't stumble and God forbid act upon one. Television and film that fosters fantasy and reinforces immoral norms must be avoided.

Extramarital sex has—historically—been a man's game, since the male sexual desire has been stereotypically assumed to be uncontrollable.

Yet, in a 2013 survey by the National Opinion Research Center showed that the number of married American women having affairs has nearly doubled over the last decade, much in contravention of the perceived norm. Today, 21 percent of men admit to having such affairs while 14.7 percent of women now admit to having them. The actual number is presumed to be significantly higher. What does this say to the moral char-acter of our society? Sadly, this phenomenon is present in our religious communities as well even among those who claim to embrace the centrality of the Ten Commandments and to love their life partners.

From a religious perspective, an honest and loving marriage is central to the continuance of the Jewish faith. The perpetuation of the ancient values consecrated between the marriage of the spiritual and mundane is paramount. Violating these norms perverts the sacred duty we are tasked with during our temporal existence. Thus, we have to do all we can to preserve the collaborative holy covenant that strengthens our families and our society.

To avoid the consequences of a society that turns a blind eye to the normalization of adultery, we have to be cognizant to protect our own marriages. Adultery, as one of many causes of failed marriages, must be rejected through the dual tasks of ethical conviction and spiritual commitment. We must cultivate moral accountability, caring for our spouses and children legitimately, and upholding the Jewish commitment to monogamy and the shared covenant of love and devotion.

3.
CAN WE RESURRECT THE VIRTUE OF FRIENDSHIP IN OUR TIME?

In our modern times, the notions of what constitutes true friendship have been heavily altered by the prominence of online media. Flesh and blood relationships have been substituted for digital companionship; "friends" are no harder to find than by a simple request and a click. As a society, what have we to gain by this commodification of friendship? Has the goal of gaining hundreds, thousands, and, in some cases, even millions of "friends" disrupted the ancient definitions of human relationships? Such a notion strikes at the heart of the contemporary human condition: abstracted pixels on a computer versus interpersonal development and growth. Our existential quest, then, is to transcend the distractions of meaningless digital ephemera that have become our companions and regain the virtues of true friendship.

The first existential dilemma we find in recorded spiritual history is a profound one. During the creation of humanity itself, God sees that man is lonesome and declares that "It is not good for man to be alone." From the beginning of existence, humans were not only physically alone but emotionally isolated and spiritually alienated. Indeed, perhaps Joseph was the loneliest: "And a man found him, when he was wandering in the field, and the man asked him, 'What are you seeking?' And he said, 'I am seeking my brothers'" (Genesis 37:15-16). This problem continues today.

We are constantly seeking our "brothers."

On a practical level, there are factors that make it more difficult today to seek out companionship. The transience of modern existence — living away from family, working longer hours, weaker social bonds exacerbated by social media's replacement of physical presence, and a consumer society that approaches relationships as transactional — aggravate the isolation. Nonetheless, researchers at the University of North Carolina have found that the number and quality of a person's social connections has a direct correlation on their long-term health. Older adults who feel socially isolated are more than twice as likely to develop high blood pressure.

What does this mean? Simple. A healthy social life is equally as important as a good diet and consistent exercise.

Rabbi Abraham Isaac Kook articulated the responsibility that Jewish values place upon seeking out our fellow for partnership and friendship. About the centrality of these relationships in human development, Rav Kook writes with clarity about finding companions within community, even amid disagreement of view:

> Part of the characteristic of Torah is that it recognizes the need for a social life with friendships, which bring to the world a good life within society. This is particularly rewarding when one's social group consists of good and scholarly people. Separation from other people and extreme asceticism, which is the approach of a significant portion of those people who, of their own, have sought closeness to Hashem, is a foreign idea to the Torah. For that reason, if one wants to acquire knowledge of Torah, he will succeed specifically by joining together with a group of learners, which shows the gains of avoiding isolation (*Ein Ayah*, *Berachot* 9:340-1).

The rabbis advised us to "acquire for yourself a friend" (*Ethics of the Fathers* 1:6). This task can be even more important than learning from teachers: "I have learned much from my teachers, but from my friends more than my teachers" (*Ta'anit* 7a). Indeed, Maimonides, who understood friendship in an Aristotelian manner (partners for our development of reason and the cultivation of virtue) explained that "man requires friends all his lifetime" (*Guide for the Perplexed*, 3:49).

Friends are not only needed for good times and for positive growth: we need friendship for perseverance and survival. Rabbi Joseph B. Soloveitchik valued both a *haver li-de'agah*—a person in whom one can confide both in times of crisis, when distress strikes, and in times of glory, when one feels happy and content—and a *haver le'de'ah*—a friend in whom he or she has absolute trust or faith, a person in whom he or she has absolute trust and faith," (Family Redeemed 27-28). Rava, a renowned talmudic sage of the fourth century, is known to have a more pithy response: "Either friendship or death" (*Ta'anit* 23a).

Rava may be correct. Studies have shown that people with the most friends (and not just relatives or children) live significantly longer than those with few friends. The friendship connected with being a couple, however, has benefits. Health-related lifestyle choices are the single major reason for sickness and death, and researchers have explored this issue. A 2015 study of more than 3,700 English couples age fifty and older published in *JAMA Internal Medicine* found the following advantages if both partners changed to a more healthy behavior (versus if only one tried to change behavior):

Men and women were at least six times more likely to quit smoking if a partner also tried to quit smoking. About two-thirds were more likely to remain physically active if joined by a partner, versus only about one-fourth who tried alone. Men and women were more than twice as likely to lose weight if a partner joined them pay it forward.

With the constant bombardment of hashtags, pins, likes, and snaps, finding value in meaningful personal relationships is of the utmost consequence to the modern condition. A simple click is no replacement for building tangible physically-present bonds. Thus, for spiritual and physical health, we should resist the current trends toward social isolation and embrace friendship. It is indispensable for the continuing progression of humanity, for bonds of friendship sustain a malnourished soul. It is our imperative to ensure that these bonds hold in perpetuity.

Like everything, investing in friendship requires discipline. This investment is crucial not only for our own survival and growth but for societal advancement.

4.
Enough With the Million Dollar Birthday Parties

When I looked at the number on the page, I thought it couldn't be true.

Not too long ago, I found myself reading an article detailing a bat mitzvah that had occurred in the New York area. While not interesting reading in and of itself, the final price tag caught my attention: a whopping $1 million.

Could this be right? Even for an extravagant party, was it necessary to spend so much?

As a rabbi who promotes various ethical-consumption initiatives, my mind couldn't comprehend the logic behind the whole endeavor. But as I thought more about the price tag, the more I began to look at other events whose cost seems to defy explanation. Fifteen thousand dollars for funeral services? Seventy-five thousand dollars for one wedding?

Life-cycle events are more important than the hedonistic, drunken festivals so many end up being. When indulgence supersedes meaning, the end result is a woeful missed opportunity to impart real meaning in some way.

Unfortunately, new social barriers often leave those with a lower socioeconomic status shamed in their more modest attempts to provide adequate celebrations for their loved ones. One of the most obscene modern life-cycle excesses occurred when Lakshmi Mittal, a billionaire steel magnate, spent about $60 million for the 2004 wedding of his daughter, including $1.5 million for wine and a reception at Versailles, the palace established by the King Louis XIV of France, who trumpeted the divine right of kings. Even after the downturn in steel prices, Mittal is still the eighth-wealthiest person from India, with a current net worth of $11.2 billion.

In contrast, India's median per capita income in 2013 was a measly $616 and is even less in mineral-rich areas. As the lawyer-filmmaker Satyabrata Dwibedy has noted, "though the eastern states possess 90 percent of the coal, iron ore, manganese and bauxite deposits, people in the region are among the poorest and getting poorer… Policies favor the vested interests of select corporations and individuals."

When we encounter these exorbitant indulgences, it should cause us to pause and reach inside ourselves to ask probing questions about the normative value of such celebrations: When did extravagance and luxury —something that can cut across all cultures, religions and creeds— become such a primary cultural value? Is debt, even potential bankruptcy for most of us trying to keep up, worth an evening of fun?

While celebratory events have the ability to enrich individuals and communities, the desire to spend lavishly for a fleeting life moment sets a noxious precedent. At times, such events can backfire on those whose narcissism becomes noxious to society.

At the close of the nineteenth century, for example, Bradley Martin and his wife, Cornelia, had followed the pattern to rise in New York's high society. They copied others by marrying their daughter to an English noble, thus acquiring a European noble title while supplying money for the English nobility to maintain their estates. Cornelia affected a hyphen in her last name to become Mrs. Bradley-Martin, and the couple periodically held massive parties.

Then the depression of 1893 resulted in massive economic hardship, the huge 1894 Pullman railroad workers' strike (their wages were cut by a third) was crushed by court injunction and President Grover Cleveland sending in federal troops, and in 1895 the Supreme Court ruled that the new income tax was unconstitutional.

Perversely, the Bradley-Martins concluded that the thing to do for the New York social season in 1897 was to hold the largest costume ball in recent history. While at first it appeared that the 700-guest event was a success, it was soon revealed that it cost $369,000. (Even when things improved somewhat in 1900, the average annual income was $438.) Feeling increasing negative attention, the Bradley-Martins left for England and Scotland and only returned once in the next fifteen years.

To be sure, weddings, birthdays, religious festivals and funerals are vital opportunities to mark growth and change for families, a time to engage with peers and celebrate a momentous occasion.

Besides the financial cost, what is the ethical cost?

I'm sure that there will be those who argue that people have the right to enjoy their wealth and spend as they please; fair point. It does not, however, address the deeper meaning of how we interact with our fellow human beings. And to me, it is abundantly clear that lavish celebrations to the point of excess are out of step with core moral values that need to be embraced.

Consider the example of Tyco CEO Dennis Kozlowski, who appeared to be doing well, with his compensation reaching $170 million in 1999. However, this was apparently not enough. In June 2001, Kozlowski threw a $2 million birthday party for his wife, a six-day extravaganza that featured Roman Empire–themed decadence. A four-hour video of the party showed young women and men barely clad, and an ice sculpture of Michelangelo's David that "urinated" vodka into glasses.

It turned out that Tyco paid about half the expense, with Kozlowski feebly maintaining that it was a business expense. Investigators then uncovered that Kozlowski had spent tens of millions of Tyco funds on apartments for himself and his wife, and he also charged his company for a $15,000 dog umbrella stand and $6,300 for a shower curtain, among other bizarre luxury items. Excesses such as this led investigators to charge Kozlowski and his chief financial officer with embezzling $170 million directly from Tyco and gaining another $430 million by illegal stock manipulation. He eventually served six and a half years in prison.

To avoid this dangerous trend from escalating, we have to reinvest societal capital toward the twin virtues of modesty and moderation. I have too often witnessed superficiality being substituted for meaning-making. Family and friends should remind loved ones that what is most important when creating a major life event is bringing people together under a banner of love and partnership, rather than one-upmanship and petty attention-seeking.

Those who are concerned with the trend of expressing love through consumerism should consider alternative models, shifting the focus of life-cycle celebrations from materialism and extravagance to a more general spiritual and ethical approach.

Pride in hosting a humble gathering leaves a longer-lasting happy memory than an overly saccharine and ephemeral bacchanal. A modest event that honors workers, animals and the environment through consumption choices while also raising funds for those in need is an inspiring way to model one's values.

Otherwise, we culturally exclude others who are less fortunate and leave them open to isolation and embarrassment.

So where does real value stem? Instead of inciting competition—possibly even animosity—with our neighbors, it is an imperative that we should work toward creating celebrations that are *expressive* rather than *expensive*. Celebrations that foster inclusiveness and community-building will do so much more for participants than being another opportunity to take advantage of complimentary food and swag. Instead of an overblown affair, hosts should be encouraged to bring their own creative energies and new perspectives for their guests to enjoy.

For the life of me, I can't find a justification for a million-dollar celebration, whether it be a birthday, a bar mitzvah, a *quinceañera* or even a wedding or a funeral. What should tie people to one another during momentous occasions should be humility and love, not wealth and hollowness.

Because, in the end, an extravagant party is hollow, a shell that possibly masks an inner insecurity. By having the strength to look beyond the glamour, we can be better equipped to find the beauty of a humble celebration that can bring about the most precious moments in our life.

5.
Bringing Kindness Into the Workplace

My first job out of college was at a major corporation. I was only spoken to when I was needed for a task. There was no community, no warmth, no love. I felt like a cog, akin to something out of Lang's *Metropolis*; a mere component of a cold machine. After a few months, I ran for the hills, never to return to a similar workplace.

For the past generation, there has been a persistent corporate measuring of "winners and losers," divided solely by those who have money and those who do not, with the assumption that it is natural for the "losers" to fall by the wayside. (This mindset was exemplified most remarkably during the primaries for President during the 2016 election cycle.) The law of the jungle appears to be not only inevitable, but desirable. Americans are burnt out from working so hard. Our workforce is becoming increasingly competitive, demanding, and draining. From morning rush hour until beyond the end of the workday, the motto seems to be: "Nice guys finish last."

Those demands aren't going to change any time soon, but what if we injected a bit more kindness into our work environment, so that we did not have such an ingrained "dog eat dog" atmosphere?

In the summer of 2013, scholars from diverse backgrounds met at Stanford University to discuss the notion of compassion in the workplace. Business graduate Dr. Olivia O'Neill noted that "people are particularly likely to catch the emotions of their leaders." Thus, if a CEO is particularly lacking in compassion, this will filter down to the employees, and will increase the tendency toward employee burnout, which will hurt the company's performance. At the conference, Stanford Assistant Professor of Psychology Jamil Zaki stated that companies tend to follow a policy of "attention, selection, and attrition," so if a company has compassion it will likely attract employees who are kind and generous, fostering cooperation. National University of Singapore Business School Associate Professor Jayanth Narayanan pointed out that, in spite of the belief that forgiveness shows weakness, we admire many leaders such as those who chose forgiveness over vengeance, Monandas Gandhi and Nelson Mandela for example. Professor Kristin Neff of the University of Texas discussed her research, which demonstrated that, contrary to what many in management believe, overwhelmingly negative feedback does not motivate employees. Rather than leading to more productivity, constant negative feedback leads to a defensive response; employees respond much better to feedback that is three- to five-times more positive than negative. In addition to being a moral decision, compassion in the work-place may be a strategic move as well. Several years ago, the *New York Times* reported that kindness increases productivity in profound ways:

Researchers at Wharton, Yale and Harvard have figured out how to make employees feel less pressed for time: force them to help others. According to a recent study, giving workers menial tasks or, surprisingly, longer breaks actually leads them to believe that they have less time, while having them write to a sick child, for instance, makes them feel more in control and 'willing to commit to future engagements despite their busy schedules.' The idea is that completing an altruistic task increases your sense of productivity, which in turn boosts your confidence about finishing everything else you need to do.

There are signs of positive change. Surveys of millennials tend to show that a majority do not want the traditional high salary corporate job, with one study showing that 74 percent expressed a preference for working collaboratively in small groups. A startup company dedicated to exploring societal issues in new ways, Creating the Future, has embraced the principles of compassion, making it the responsibility of all to look out for one another: "…It is our collective responsibility to figure out how to support and bring out the best in that person and the situation." Thus, employees who feel burnout will be treated with compassion instead of being cast out as useless drones; this is an experiment worth emulating.

I often think back to how spiritually drained I felt when I left work each night from my cold corporate position. I wasn't empowered enough to inject acts of proactive kindness into the workplace. Now, however, I realize how many people suffer in their day jobs—living to work rather than working to live—only to come home to stressful domestic and family demands. To reverse the trend, each of us— in our way—can make a difference by making our workplace a more enjoyable, warm, and thoughtful environment.

The Torah fervently stressed the importance of honoring the dignity of workers and the rabbinic tradition went even further to tell stories of righteous people who helped their employees and co-workers:

Every day, all the other workers and I pool our food, and eat it. But today, I saw that there was one man who had no bread and he was ashamed. So I told all the other men, 'Today, I will collect the food.' When I came to that man, I pretended to take bread from him, so that he should not be ashamed (*Shabbat*, 156b)

As Jews and as conscientious people, we must serve as model employers and co-workers teaching that the workplace is not merely a place to make money but a place to build compassionate relationships. Those bonds will not only improve our quality of work but will enhance the workplace to be a place of dignity.

6.
ARE WE RESPONSIBLE FOR ONE ANOTHER?

What is the core essence of Judaism? Is it primarily a personal religious conviction or a communal one? Is it a series of epistemological contentions, or an emotional journey? To be sure, these rhetorical questions are never-ending and are at the heart of our great tradition. Learning how to reconcile these different ideals into a common reality is enough to warrant a call to action toward the grand notion of *arvut*, that we are responsible for one another.

Jews are vital in the spiritual enterprise of learning the values imbued by Torah. The Sages taught that a wise individual is someone who can learn from anyone (*Avot* 4:1), and in their consummate wisdom of the enigmatic, the Kabbalists taught that every Jew represents a single letter of Torah. Thus, although we may be individuated with distinct personalities, wants and desires, at some point, we all converge as a great nation. We are crucial to the spiritual development of our fellow, though we may not always know it.

But we are not limited to our ideals alone. To sustain spiritual growth, so vital to the health of the soul (if not the body), people have to journey beyond familiar comforts. Responsibility toward humanity means taking up the critical mantle of creating communities where there are gaps, filling the vacuum with respect for the inherent dignity of all people regardless of status or station. Pluralistic understanding is the key, though disagreements will surely arise. Being aware of this means that building communities is not dependent on picayune differences of ideology or ritual (let's say), but on mutual regard for deeply held convictions. For even if we do not agree with one other, the shared destiny of the Jewish people rests on the sacred integrity and wisdom that has been cultivated for countless generations.

Modernity, indeed post-modernity, raised serious questions about our role in caring for one another. The increasingly prominent role of digital anonymity has created a sense of distance in human interactions, nearly to the point of abstraction. But people aren't made of bits of code. The blood and sinew that was created from upon High binds our collective fates, and it can inspire us to reflect on the monumental role we have to play in stewarding succeeding epochs of humanity toward the path that is most just. For without this in mind, we doom ourselves to irrelevancy and the void of indifference. This is the antithesis of *arvut*, the antithesis of leading a life guided by Torah values.

We have been chosen for a singular and crucial mission: to bring holiness to the world. The task, though immense, is part and parcel of the Divine contract that was struck by our ancestors eons ago with the Divine. To fulfill the terms, we must be absolutely unequivocal about our commitment to respect, to tolerance, to the perspicacity we need to ensure that all people, not only Jews, can thrive in the world. It is our eternal task, it is our constant spiritual test. And perhaps, it is our most important link to all of creation.

The primary value that should guide every agency here in our community is *arvut*. We are diverse, and thus we will have different views; nonetheless, we must take care of one another.

7.
WELCOMING YOUNG LEADERS TO BOARDS

As an educator and social activist, I am always impressed when people begin to see shortcomings in their own community and begin to mobilize their untapped potential to create meaningful change. Since I moved to Phoenix, I've seen underdeveloped young talent grow in step with the burgeoning needs of a growing young community.

Over the course of my experience leading the Start Me Up! Fellowship, the first cohort of the Jewish Leadership Corps and the first Honeymoon Israel trip, I've been exposed to a vast amount of raw talent on display from young people from all over our community.

Their backgrounds are varied and their experiences so diverse that, collectively, they impress me with their vast range of knowledge and insight. These young professionals—between 22 and 40 years old—are filled with fresh ideas and interesting perspectives on how to move the Jewish community forward into the future. They are optimistic and creative.

It has become apparent to me that the voices of young people have too often been ignored by institutions entrenched with keeping the status quo. To sustain our community for the future, we can do better. There is an undeniable trend that many nonprofits and corporations tend to retain members of their boards for indefinite amounts of time, causing organizations to become stagnant with the engine of uniformity. When this occurs, no bold ideas will emerge or be discussed, and everything will remain business as usual.

When business-as-usual becomes the norm, members of the community are not inspired to reach beyond the possible. Indeed, this model of generational intransigence has the effect of doing the complete opposite. So how are our communities going to utilize this latent pool of enthusiastic talent?

One of the most effective means to spur innovation, whether at the local or global level, is to include those same young professionals on nonprofit boards. There is much to be gained by inclusion of young people at the top echelons of leadership. Seniors in our community can bring decades of rich valuable experience that we must cherish. Others, with much less experience, bring fresh ideas and approaches never considered before in the community.

This is what's needed more than ever for our growing Jewish community: empowering a diversity of expertise and of wisdom to be dreamers and builders. Some need to learn humility to step back and empower others, while others need to learn to take initiative and to step forward. Those with more experience should reach out to mentor those new to community leadership.

Though there may be some reticence to have someone with less outright life experience become a member of a board, what is gained is infinitely valuable. Most importantly, when these young people are asked to join a board, the entire dynamic of the board can be revitalized and changed in a positive manner if the board members and team dynamic are cultivated. Indeed, a new manner of expertise is introduced. The perspectives that are brought onto the board from people who have more current awareness of technological and social trends amplifies outreach capability, which in turn brings more attention to the needs of the target population (opening up vital channels to new networks), which will invite curious people to investigate what is happening in the community.

I would like to urge the many boards of our greater Jewish community—synagogues, schools and nonprofits—to consider adding talented young people to their rosters. It is for their benefit to have more than one token young board member without serious responsibilities and leadership development opportunities. In addition to age diversity, we should commit to ideological diversity, diverse skill sets, engaging personality types and gender parity (with women often grossly underrepresented on staffs and boards).

Every board has different needs, but each can do better in achieving balance and parity. Our lay leaders ready to roll up their sleeves should be cherished, nourished and cultivated! We need diversity, not only for our results-driven ends, but also for our holiness process. A just and holy community engages all kinds of people in leadership. The Jewish community is sitting on a gold mine, only waiting for the right people to step up and take advantage of its bounty.

8.
The Emotional Roller Coaster of Fostering a Child

We knew it wouldn't be easy and yet we knew we felt called to this. While it's difficult to raise any infant, we were prepared for that challenge. What's more difficult is to be prepared for a life-altering waiting game. Will the child who we have come to love so dearly stay permanently with our family or return to someone in his biological family? The process of fostering a child is akin to the movements of a roller coaster: there are harrowing turns and loops, sudden starts and stops, but there is also exhilaration and excitement at the prospects for the future.

The ascending climb, so steeped with the fear of anticipation and worry, is so tangible, so present in the process of fostering a vulnerable child. And in that part of the process, not knowing if your foster child will stay or go is mentally and spiritually taxing. It's taxing on your nerves, it's taxing on your spouse, your biological children, but, foremost, it's taxing on foster child who is getting more and more attached to you each day. While, in theory, reunification with biological family is considered the best, in some cases, foster parents can have their doubts. These unforeseen bumps place an unbelievable burden of stress on the part of the foster family. Indeed, to hand over a child to family that a baby doesn't know, a family that, one hopes, is equipped to share love and support is nonetheless a scary prospect.

The need for our collective participation is so urgent. According to statistics from Administration for Children and Families, a part of the De-partment of Healthy and Human Services, it was estimated that Child Protective Service units across the nation received 3.6 million referrals, which involved approximately 6.6 million children. Of these children, only about 150,000 of them will be placed in foster homes and only 50,000 will end up being adopted. Nearly a quarter of them will develop long-term Post-Traumatic Stress Disorder, a fifth will be homeless by adulthood, 71 percent of the young women will be pregnant before 21 and over a half will be unemployed by age 24. So much needless suffering. So much wasted potential; the stomach-dropping bumps of an unsteady track.

The consequences of being raised in a broken home are real for so many children—too many—and the effects not only stunt the development of these innocent souls, they affect the economic and social bonds that bring our nation together. If you don't grow up in a home with a loving family, then your chances at success in life are so much dimmer. We want to help give children their best start in life; to shoot for the stars! I believe we owe the emotional discomfort bringing these unfamiliar children into our care. As hard as that is, the alternative of children having no loving home in the interim is never a good option. We don't have children to gain in some way or with some expectation that it'll be easy. Rather, we take care of vulnerable children—those we gave birth to and those we've brought in to foster or adopt—because it is the greatest moral obligation and spiritual privilege we are charged to fulfill. To ensure every child is loved!

In my personal life, I've been blessed to see the wonders of welcoming a foster child in my home. My wife, though often heroically exhausted by the rigors of caring for this defenseless baby, is an inspiration for giving this non-biological child all the love she gives to our birth children. To be sure, our kids are learning that our home is not just a private place, but also a space where we collaborate to nurture the vulnerable. I pray they will pass along this value to their children as well. What a ride that would be!

Conclusion

Contemporary Jewish leadership requires several key components: commitment to a handful of values, core competencies in the language of consequential action, and the pursuit of justice in all of its form. There is much at stake as we strive to improve our communities, support the vulnerable, and create a more unprejudiced, egalitarian world. The process of our leadership centers around uniting community. To do so, we must raise the bar—individually and collectively—always holding ourselves to ethical standards beyond repute, cultivating a leadership that ensures we move away from simple good deeds and actions towards tangible, moral results.

In the twenty-first century, Jewish ethics has to be applied in ways that go beyond the routine. If we are to succeed in the constant battle between what is easy and what is just, we have to rise and meet the complexity of interconnected, intersectional challenges. This is arduous, this is stressful. But what in life isn't? Our foremost concern in is the ethical, which, in general, is concerned with the interactions between people. Jewish ethics—or even looking broader to the spectrum of interfaith-based moral decision-making—demands inclusion of a Divine constituent. Accepting a place for a Divine role in social change and moral development ensures that we envelop ourselves in the most significant part of our faith.

To embrace the full essence of Jewish ethics, we need to shake ourselves from the torpor that modern society uses to seduce us into complacency. The overexposure of celebrity, political horse races, and disposable gossip has seemingly replaced much of the time society used to dedicate to civil education, nuance. In that void is where our task becomes absolutely clear, and were each of us is called upon to exercise leadership. By this, I mean that limiting the amount of inconsequential pabulum is an essential part of shedding the vagaries of our modern media culture. When we look back at what we have accomplished, knowing that we have eschewed these distractions will go far in changing the attitude of approaching our tasks with full clarity and commitment.

Naturally, this is the challenge Judaism advances to the modern soul: To be spiritually connected to the mysteries of existence and to the empyrean realm, as well as being responsible for the state of the world as it is presently. If we are to be stewards of the better world we imagine for ourselves, our children and grandchildren, then we are to be realists and idealists, activists and dreamers. There are many different kinds of leaders, different leadership traits, and different processes of leadership. Ultimately, one must be authentic to their values, personality, and social change philosophy.

Personally, I'm most inspired by stories that touch upon the complexity of the human spirit: the triumph over adversity, the weak prevailing against the strong, the community coming together for a common cause; the stuff of Norman Rockwell's *oeuvre*. I look for the people who run towards obstacles, those who commit their lives to serving others, who take care of others at great expense—financially and physically—to themselves. To discover these hidden treasures, we have to first search for the fires in our own soul. Our objectives in this life can't be sustained on artificiality, on lackadaisical activism. No! The goal is to give back and do our hardest work, pouring out every last drop of positive energy in service of reaching that ultimate inspirational moment.

Our bodies instinctively seek warmth and safety. We yearn for comfort, because the moment we step out of our comfort zone—our freshly made bed, a steamy shower—the world becomes unrelenting and harsh; that is simply how the world operates. The art of living in an inspired way is learning how to keep our inspiration levels at a sustained level so that, while we may find our tasks formidable and onerous, we are never discouraged from our tasks at hand. Keeping those holy sparks inside of us lit is the primary task of our mission.

At the same time, we have to be cognizant that being involved in community leadership can be thankless and endlessly challenging. There are sections of each community that want their particular needs met before any other. Balancing competing populations of influence is delicate. That is why our focus needs to be on the most vulnerable, rather than on the most powerful. Those of this latter camp can always be attended to with little consequence to their privileged station in society. But those who aren't always heard by leading political or social leaders need priority. Otherwise, who will speak for them? Understanding the plight of the weak, the tired, those yearning to breathe freely, are of the utmost importance. It is the obligation of those who truly seek to meld leadership with meaningful social justice action to take up causes that empower those who struggle to power themselves. That is true leadership.

When I see problems in the world, I am empowered by the words of Torah, of the stories of our ancestors who sought a better world for all of humanity. They faced challenges we can hardly fathom. Nonetheless, we take up their models of righteousness and search for ways to apply them to the modern world. While the ancient paradigms may not, at first glance, explicitly fit into the mindset of the twenty-first century activist, they are nonetheless the central teachings that I look to before embarking on any project.

When we find those teachers and philosophies that inspire us, we have to hold them dear to our hearts. Learning to generate inspiration wherever we are—in life, in location—can only be achieved when a proper frame of mind frame is discerned. So then, let us take the inspiration that comes our way, and the vast wisdom of Jewish tradition, to exercise leadership *together* in order to create a more just and holy world.

It is our test, it is our our task.

It is our dream.

Let us make that dream tangible so that the world may flourish in peace, holiness, and justice.

ABOUT THE AUTHOR

Rabbi Dr. Shmuly Yanklowitz is the President & Dean of Valley Beit Midrash, Founder & President of Uri L'Tzedek, and Founder & CEO of The Shamayim V'Aretz Institute.

Rabbi Yanklowitz's writings have appeared in outlets as diverse as the *New York Times*, the *Wall Street Journal*, and the *Atlantic*, among many other secular and religious publications. Rabbi Yanklowitz is a sought-after educator, social justice activist, and motivational speaker on the subjects of Jewish spirituality and ethics.

Rabbi Shmuly earned a masters degree from Harvard University in Leadership and Psychology, another masters from Yeshiva University in Jewish Philosophy, and a doctorate from Columbia University in Moral Development and Epis-temology. He obtained rabbinical ordination from the Yeshivat Chovevei Torah Rabbinical School and two additional, private ordinations in Israel. He has twice been named one of America's Top Rabbis by *Newsweek*. In 2016, *The Forward* named Rabbi Shmuly one of "The Most Inspiring Rabbis in America." In the same year, Yanklowitz was selected for the Ariane de Rothschild Fellowship in Cross-Cultural Leadership and Innovative Entrepreneurship at the University of Cambridge.

As an activist and educator, Rabbi Yanklowitz has volunteered, staffed trips, and taught across the world, including Israel, Ghana, India, France, Thailand, El Salvador, England, Senegal, Germany, Switzerland, Ukraine, Argentina, South Africa, and Haiti. Rabbi Dr. Yanklowitz has also served as a rabbinic representative, facilitator, and speaker at the World Economic Forum in Geneva and Davos.

Rabbi Shmuly, his wife Shoshana, and their two children live in Scottsdale, Arizona.

Visit Rabbi Shmuly at www.rabbishmuly.com

Facebook - www.facebook.com/RabbiShmulyYanklowitz
Twitter - @RavShmuly

In Loving memory of Robert C. Frost ז״ל

*From Robin, AJ,
and all their loving family & friends*

*GONE
BUT NOT FORGOTTEN*